The Anthropology of Sex

The Anthropology of Sex

ABEL JEANNIERE

TRANSLATED BY JULIE KERNAN

WITH A FOREWORD BY DAN SULLIVAN

HARPER & ROW, PUBLISHERS

NEW YORK, EVANSTON, AND LONDON

IMPRIMI POTEST: Phil. Laurent, praep. prov. Paris

IMPRIMATUR: 24 June, 1964, Jean Hottot, v. g.

FIRST EDITION

LIBRARY OF CONGRESS CATALOG CARD NUMBER: 67-14941

D-R

FOREWORD

Jeannière, a theological anthropologist, sees his task as one of "interpreting love beyond the schemas and stereotypes of (male-female) 'natures' in the truth and freedom of personal relations." His daring lies in this steady insistence that human sex can never be grasped in terms of fixed and statically complementary male and female gender roles. Instead, human sex must be approached as an integral part of a dynamic, open-ended person-to-person history. It is only in this lived history that human sex reveals itself as "being-for-the-other" and as "a constitutive ingredient of the human person." We can recall, by way of contrast, that in Sartre the lovers remain ultimately apart and even antagonistic individuals, as a result of becoming objects of one another's imperialistic subjectivity. Jeannière, however, sees authentically transcending subjectivity and freedom as depending solely on the creation of the we-subject. Isolated individuality is impossible according to him because, from the first, man and woman are not just "comparable to one another but (still) different and independent," they are not merely "proximate realities," they are in no sense "separate" individuals. Only the relation is given. No other principle of explanation can be introduced, such as reproduction, or sexual polarity or complementarity, for these only tend to make the relation as such extraneous to the person.[1]

One of the more far-reaching effects of this position, which the author only mentions in passing, is to give to the sexual aspect of human history this history's own dynamism; sexual love can then no longer be judged inimical to either human creativity or spiritual freedom. In fact, as Jeannière states, "one of the craftiest and most baneful ways of denying that there is a human history" is to regard human sex as based on and defined by the "immutable natures" of

[1] John Macmurray, "Chastity," in his *Reason and Emotion* for a similar idea.

5

the masculine and feminine. Polarizing human sexuality amounts to a "nascent naturalism" which may pretend to the world that the man-woman relation is humanly fulfilling, but which really regards conjugal love as the death of spiritual life, because sex itself has been reduced to the determinisms of bodily conformations. To lay the groundwork for harmony between human sex and spiritual freedom is a major advance over the past where men have traditionally sung the sailor's mournful refrain, about "answering the call of the open sea and leaving the thing I most adore, my darling wife, Nancy." Other readers may think of Claudel's *The Tidings Brought to Mary*, or again of Eliot's *Cocktail Party*, where the protagonists are led by grace or the pall of domesticity into the open sea of spiritual adventure and a deeper, more satisfying inner unity, by going beyond or forsaking sex and the man-woman relation. Innumerable artists and writers, philosophers and theologians, have felt compelled to warn us that spiritual creativity can be affirmed only *against* woman-flesh. But as Jeannière reminds us again, "in man's relation with woman, Marx makes the relation to the other as man . . . the very measure of humanization attained in relation to nature." In other words, spiritual freedom and human creativity are themselves numbed and mutilated to the extent that they are flights from the man-woman relation, because this is flight from one's self, one's being-for-the-other. "To be fully oneself," Jeannière repeats again and again, "is to know that one is for the other." To flee from woman-as-flesh is like using her as-flesh; subsequent freedom and creativity will not escape the shadow of this negation.

Some readers may feel baffled to find Jeannière, a French priest, ignoring Christian tradition concerning sex in favor of a phenomenological approach which involves an intuitive grasp of the essential structure and connections of sex as immediately given in our language and in what is called "consciousness-of." There is a clear tension in the author's thought between the task of uncovering the meaning of Eros and of continually affirming that it is part of an open-ended and indefinable human history. To give context to Jeannière's position, it seems necessary to divide it under three headings: Woman, Love, and Sexuality.

WOMAN

Twenty years have passed since Simone de Beauvoir published *The Second Sex*. Its main theses have been depressingly confirmed by continuously accumulating anthropological and psychological evidence that the female sex is the archetypal instance of economic colonialism and social *apartheid*. Psychoanalysis has gone far in clarifying some of the ingredients of authentic personhood, such as the "existential" concepts of self-love and self-criticism and the more classic categories of choice and learning. It has all confirmed de Beauvoir's partly autobiographical insights into how woman is unconscionably dissociated and destroyed by the images connected with the Eternal Feminine. It should have been obvious long ago that the essentially passive and decorative correlates of the Eternal Feminine can engender nothing in woman except self-ignorance and self-doubt of a purely impotent sort. Woman's condition must not only reason throughout the mother-child relation and conjugal life, but through them into man's political, social, religious, and intellectual life, infecting each of these spheres with overtones of the ironic and tragic.[2]

The question of human sex, then, is not only a question of the history of the man-woman relation but, more precisely, of woman's relation to herself. For it is as an individual person, Jeannière notes, that woman must retain that mystery which is the food of love. To understand the full importance of this view, we need only recall that no great thinker, from Aristotle to Freud, has written anything that touches even remotely on the meaning of life, love, and the person apart from the living memory of his personal encounters with woman, as mother, wife, or lover. One would think this a mere truism if it were not that we are constantly asked to believe that particular conceptions of human nature, or even of human sex, have their genesis in speculative dialectics more or less untouched by some sort of intimacy with alienated woman. For example, no serious commentator I know has traced Freud's highly mechanistic and subpersonal conception of libidinal energy

[2] Augustine, Nietzsche, Unamuno, and Freud are examples.

as much to his personal history as to academic influences, such as that of Helmholtz's positivism. But in fact, I would think Freud's conception of both libido and love would have been utterly different had his mother loved and treated *all* her children equally, rather than singling Sigmund for what he must have somewhere known was an impersonal and suffocating special "affection." This early experience was repeated in Freud's notably unhappy marriage, which left him with his ironic type of misogynism, and with an "objective" attitude to romantic love as "the overestimation of the sexual object"—a phrase we would hardly expect to find on the lips of a satisfied lover.

The Christian tradition, which Jeannière shares, also bears witness to the close connection between theory of sex and theory of woman. Thomas Aquinas, for example, having already agreed with Aristotle that woman was a "defective and misbegotten" man, "an incidental being," both spiritually and physically man's inferior (an opinion shared by a recent Catholic encyclopedia)—Thomas could go on to agree with St. Augustine that "nothing so casts down the manly mind from its heights as the fondling of women" (*Summa Theol.*, II,II,151,3). To some Christians, "feminality" has seemed only half a step removed from bestiality, and the celibate priestly tradition can hardly be appreciated apart from endlessly echoed warnings, such as St. John Damascene's, that woman is "the advance outpost of hell." So long as woman, the goal of man's sexual desire, is, or is prejudged to be, inauthentically human or unworthy of total love and self-abandon, no metapsychology, or philosophical anthropology, is likely to see sexual desire as a wholly personal passion, or man himself as anything but inwardly divided and alienated. One need only imagine how, had St. Augustine's common-law wife been to him a full equal, intellectually and spiritually, the course of Christian spirituality and psychology would have gone.[3] Or, had Freud remained the ardent lover of his earlier letters to his fiancée, one could imagine psychoanalysis having a slower but far more human beginning

Jeannière could have found many precedents in the mainstream

[3] Dan Sullivan, "Why There Has Never Been a Great Woman Philosopher," *Review of Metaphysics*, XVI (March 1963), pp. 559–63.

of contemporary Christian theology for bestowing an initial approval on woman's changing role in society, only to warn her at the end against being "masculinized" and thus losing her "true nature." But Jeannière's thought is purged of that neomisogynistic jargon of "psychic complementarity." Following de Beauvoir, he acknowledges that woman, not man, is often a better criterion of the "human" because she has been spared so many of the self-alienating aggressive roles enjoined by the Eternal Masculine. But he knows that woman has been mutilated by her vastly more stereotyped and limiting gender role. Among Christian thinkers, he is almost alone in answering to the question "What is woman?" that it "is impossible to distinguish between nature and culture," but "woman in herself does not exist," and "there is no Eternal Feminine." Christian readers may wonder if woman does not have a special "vocation" for either "real or sublimated motherhood." But Jeannière regards allocating a special psychic "function" to either sex as curtailing and prejudging human freedom, and asks why woman should be singled out as being any more *for* motherhood than man is spoken of as being *for* fatherhood. In a flat declaration apt to shock many readers, Jeannière says: "It is only history that divides the couple's inseparable parenthood into (the roles of) paternity and maternity."

This position does not imply a total divorce of body and mind, but only that, from an evolutionary standpoint, and following philosophers like Merleau-Ponty, Jeannière believes that the human level *restructures* what it absorbs from the preceding biological level. "In the transition from the biological to the human, it is the human that gives meaning." Woman's freedom from the very start is more decisive than her biochemistry or anatomy in determining what she makes of herself as a person. Only early and continued stereotyping by social images can block and frustrate her given freedom. To define a human being, says Jeannière, in terms of hormones, glands, and genital apparatus is "drearily materialistic. . . . Why should organs or gametes define a temperament? . . . . The biological condition of existence can in no wise define a free appraisal of one's relation to the world and to one's own ego." To genitalize a psychology of polarized "natures" in terms of concepts like "welcome" and "possession" is only to testify to the persisting influence of socially stereotyped "images which underlie the traditional conceptions."

Jeannière refers explicitly to studies made in France, showing the early age at which sexual stereotyping takes place. He observes, for example, how often the little boy is asked, "What will you be when you grow up," while the little girl's destiny is implicitly settled by remarks about her "prettiness." But it is possible that Jeannière is unaware of recent work in America and Britain that sets the age when sexual stereotyping begins at about eighteen months, and sees the process completed, with the sexual image fixed, at between two and a half and three years. The studies of Hampson and Money at Johns-Hopkins University, and a parallel study at Leeds University, go even further and declare that this sexual self-image is exceedingly plastic or arbitrary: boys or girls dressed and treated as members of the opposite sex (usually in cases where parents or guardians were determined to have the other sex) during the early months of their lives and until about the age of three, will manifest permanently all the psychological characteristics of the *learned sex*. Rather amazingly, this learning is so fixed that both study groups ended by recommending that, where it is feasible, surgery and hormone therapy to fit the genital sex to the learned, psychological sex is less disturbing to the child than trying to revert its self-image back to the other sex.[4] Thus, classic studies such as Terman's and Erikson's, purporting to find "given" psychic "natures" in four- and five-year-old children which fully demarcate them sexually, would seem now to be inconclusive. Hampson and Money have admittedly dealt with abnormal children, but they have nevertheless indicated that the question of any male or female "nature" should at least be left open.

But Jeannière does not think that the body-difference counts

[4] J. L. Hampson, and Joan Hampson, "The Ontogenesis of Sexual Behavior in Man," in *Sex and Internal Secretions*, W. C. Young, ed. (3d ed.; Baltimore: Williams & Wilkins, 1961), Vol. 2, pp. 1401–32; J. Money, J. G. Hampson, and J. L. Hampson, "Imprinting and the Establishment of Gender Role," in *A.M.A. Arch. Neuro. Psychiat.*, 77 (1957), pp. 333–36; J. W. Money, "Sex Hormones and Other Variables in Human Eroticism," in *Sex and Internal Secretions*, cited above, pp. 1383–1400. Cf. also their publications in *Bull. Johns-Hopkins Hosp.* 96 (1955).

for absolutely nothing, psychologically and socially. While he feels that the man-woman relation must be counted as a "mobile genesis," the individual's existence, contrary to Sartre, is never a pure "project." Sexual differentiation is not one of mere social "contingency." In the man-woman relation, "despite the shift in roles and the mutations in values, we are not dealing with a societal creation." But Jeannière is not trying to resurrect the gender roles. He notes, first, that certain social roles can become integrated in one's historical nature, and be fulfilling rather than alienating. Such, often, is motherhood. Beyond this, man and woman are distinguished in two ways: first, woman's eroticism involves more of her whole body, while the boy's is chiefly phallic; this, says Jeannière, leads to woman's pride and anxieties being focused on her whole behavior, while man's is focused on his virility; and second, pregnancy makes its subject more vulnerable and dependent, which society must and does acknowledge. I would comment, however, that the absence of a clitoral or phallic-type eroticism in girls is apt to reflect the greater burden of puritanism borne by women, and also the fact that, at a much deeper level, she cannot find images of herself in the world that would correspond with and justify her "projecting" herself into life in a "virile" way as person. Similarly with the boy, greater bodily eroticism might easily be his lot if masculine stereotypes were more physically affectionate, if he were allowed to develop the passive side of his nature and not forced to project himself against the world, and if he were allowed to develop the sort of "polymorphously perverse" body-integrity described by contemporary psychological theorists.[5]

LOVE

To say that romantic love between man and woman, understood as the ground of sexual union and abandon, nevertheless goes deeper and extends beyond the erotic, is not necessarily to make a distinction between Eros and Agape. Sexual desire and human desire are, in my opinion, one and the same, with different

[5] Especially Norman Brown, Herbert Marcuse, Alan Watts.

moments only. In fact, the traditional understanding of Agape in God as a pure and disinterested bestowal probably stemmed as much from theologians' fear of a "sexy" God, as from the philosophical notion of God as pure Act. Thus, Jeannière rightly talks about love as a propensity in man's nature; man simply cannot *not* love, and he must love "fully." Man must love because it is only there that, as Hegel observed, the mind "feels its own unity." And as Jeannière reminds us, pointing us back to the delirium of that "unreal" state called "being in love," "every person learning to love knows that he is himself only with the other," and, "for the lover there is no refuge in himself; he is truly what he is only before the other." I love, therefore I am, to paraphrase Descartes, or as Marx added, it is the sexual relation "which first really teaches man to believe in the objective world outside himself." If *I* am, the world must be.

An important and paradoxical aspect of love, Jeannière tells us, is that the "elect," or beloved, while confirming us in the freedom of our being-for-the-other, at the same time *compels* us to love. There is thus a double compulsion: to love, and to *fall* in love. "We do not choose to love; we capitulate before love." Jeannière notes a further contradiction in love, that while it is only love that establishes and individuates the self in a unique way as being-for-the-other, it is the *given* individuality of the beloved which elicits the "falling." "An androgynous unity is by no means the vow made by persons in love." What they fall for is the mystery of the individual person; lovers are not mechanically seeking a male or female complement, as many Jungians would have us believe, but the other as unique *person*. Lovers desire "a union in what is particular and unique to each" as persons, and it is "the very individuality of each of two human beings that becomes a source of happiness to the other, for their union is based on this individuality . . . (which) makes them mysterious to each other, mysterious as the source of life itself."[6]

One of the effects of falling in love is to confirm man's finitude, but as a finitude already transcending itself in the other. Love

[6] William Earle, "Love and Metaphysics," in *Experience, Existence and the Good*, I. C. Lieb, ed. (Southern Illinois Univ. Press, 1961, pp. 49–68.)

makes me not only "search elsewhere than within" for what I need, but also promises me a "response." Such a radical dependence on the other causes many of us, Jeannière observes, to seek a way into self-autonomy through various causes and careers. "Sacrifices for an ideal or for the future conceal from us our fear of casting ourselves into the waves of a great passion where man is metamorphosed." But by recognizing that they are nothing "except by and for the other," lovers mutually constitute each other's true autonomy and transcending worth at the moment of constituting a "we." It is this lived juxtaposition of freedom-through-falling that leads Jeannière to reject Sartre's description of the lovers' relation as "a play of impenetrable mirrors" or a "momentary forgetting of solitude in the mists of tenderness." There can be neither freedom nor transcendence apart from intimacy. (If one reads Sartre carefully, one is struck by the failure to carry his brilliant description of intimacy through to many of the specific causes which tear it down, such as boredom.) "How," Jeannière asks Sartre, "can those who are in love lose anything of what they are on discovering that they exist through and for another?" In the original momentum of the falling, at least, "nothing else exists than this perfectible relationship."

By saying that the relation is "perfectible," Jeannière implies two things: that it is limited, but that it also has access to a "beyond," a source of further enrichment. But it is only the former aspect, the *limit* of this relation, that he carefully examines. Like most commentators, he simply sees great difficulty in romantic passion ever enduring. As the Tristan-Isolde myth shows us, he says, "It is vain to make an absolute of exceptional minutes of love . . . in which the curtain of solitude rises and the world appears for a moment as it is, simply because we ourselves arrive at what we are, that is, one being for another—even when these minutes are the only ones that give an essential zest to life." It is one of the great psychological curiosities of history that so many accept, in place of this reality so well described by Jeannière, that euphemism for a dead soul known as "conjugal affection." However, Jeannière does not go on to show us how to blunt the despair that lovers may feel when the world no longer appears as "it is." He does not show us how the mystery of the beloved's individuality can be made enduring even after the "overestimated" object is in hand, nor does he present some program or methodology for reciprocal infinitizing and perfecting of the two finite lovers. Instead, Jeannière calls upon a Kantian-type unconditional commitment to the other. "Unity is a promise that cannot be fulfilled." Thus, there must be a mutual *gratuitous* commitment, sealed before society and symbolized by the absolute giving of the bodies. The "presence" or enduring quality of human love must finally come in social terms, as "a unifying history and creator of the family community."

Does this mean that the partner must be loved gratuitously, that the absolute aspect of love must be brought in by an act of willing, or that the love which unites man and woman is basically similar to that uniting child and parent? This does indeed seem to be Jeannière's view, as it is that of many psychologists and philosophers, not to mention theologians. And it leaves room for fundamental disagreement. The love that unites the conjugal partners is, we believe, wholly different from that uniting child and parent. It calls for the continued "falling" of the lovers to be as spontaneous, as compelling, and as inevitable as during the moments of greatest "infatuation." Eros can never be gratuitous. We cannot believe that the love of the beloved must be radically less realistic than the love of self. What spiritual adviser, speaking of self-love, would tell us that it must be wholly "unreckoning," and that it "keep no score, believes all, hopes all"? Yet this is Jeannière's description of conjugal love, a self-blinding commitment that has shifted from a falling evoked by the mystery of individuality to a dutiful push from within. Real love is a critical, open-eyed, yet hopeful love; its paradigm is self-love. Because conjugal love seeks the "all," it is impossible for it to be gratuitous, that is, self-generated. To trifle with the truth about love, or about the other, kills the inner life of passion and makes the self's affectivity a grotesque "persona," or mask. If the relationship is perfectible, it is only because somewhere the individuals are not wholly and finally finite and predictable. If the aura of mystery is dispelled in love with the inevitable discovery of the other's finitude, it can be restored if the individual feels an *integrative* doubt and dissatisfaction with himself and seeks, perpetually, to create and extend his being. As Kierkegaard saw, no one need bore himself, or the other, to death. The Christian, especially, should feel both enjoined and empowered to love others as he loves himself, and as God has loved him, infinitely. Every predictable and determined facet of the self or of the beloved which seems to menace radically the mystery, spontaneity, and absoluteness of self-love or romantic love, implies to us, by the very borderline of the limit it presents, a "more," the "something beyond."[7] Thus, in our view, to expect the "All" from the other is not, as Jeannière and so many claim, to forget the other as individual, but rather the inverse: it is to remember him as self-transcending spirit, as one with constant access to an inexhaustible, personalizing Beyond, the Source of Values, God.

SEXUALITY

To understand the tension in Jeannière's position on sex, a short historical digression is necessary. There are two, perhaps three popular attitudes toward sex that reflective men have had.

Possibly the oldest way, and a perennially "new" one, is to see the sex act as a chance, or duty, to throw off one's artificial social mask and rediscover one's inner forces and feelings, at the same time uniting with a cosmic vitality, through more or less frenzied and anonymous fertility rituals. Today, this dionysian attempt at reunion with oneself and the All has psychoanalytically sophisticated advocates, among them some Christians, like Norman Brown. But a curious feature of this school, even of its Christian members, is that they do not seem to regard sexual love or acts as ever truly *personal*.

Civilized men have reacted against this dionysian, demonic abandon to body-mysticism by exalting reason and will. Self-control became the obvious corollary of control of the outer world, especially when one was goaded by reflections on man's spirit under

[7] Paul Ricoeur, *Fallible Man* (Chicago: Henry Regnery, 1965); René Le Senne, *L'Obstacle et Valeur* (Paris: Ed. Montaigne, 1932).

the impact of dreams or the visible decay of the body. But reason and will are not self-governing, as many still believe, and self-control easily slipped into body-mortification, the "death of the flesh."[8] Extreme sexual asceticism arises in history long before its philosophic elaboration by the Greeks. The Hebrew tradition, for example, is not so "earthy" and natural as many suppose, seeing often the same antagonism as did St. Paul between Eros and spiritual liberty, and allowing at times only a certain *modus vivendi* with sexual passion to those too weak to accept repression. Augustine's views of a lower, beastly nature in man were not dissimilar to those of Plato and Aristotle before him, nor to Aquinas' and Calvin's after him. It is worth emphasizing that the East, contrary to the propaganda issuing from some apologists, has been as resolutely antisexual as the West—a natural corollary of its treatment of women. Many Taoist, Hindu, and Buddhist texts are interchangeable with those of St. Jerome, with only this occasional difference: like the Manicheans, the East has found sex so expendable for the spiritual life that its use becomes wholly irrelevant—at least up to a certain stage of the ladder of perfection. Gandhi is a modern expression of the Hindu spiritualist conviction that man is divided by a lower, sexual nature.

A third attitude to sex is sometimes seen in the statement that sex is unimportant and "simply there." Many married folk fall into this category through resentment of what they consider "sexual mystiques." Detachment is popular with aesthetes like Malraux, and also with many Protestant theologians such as Tom Driver here in America.[9] This take-it-or-leave-it approach seems destined to become the position of Catholic thinkers as well, who have now grown sensitive to the charge of being unabashed materialists about sex, and who as yet appear unready to risk the path of dionysianism. What makes this attitude of detachment attractive, however, is that behind it one can retain the older attitudes of scorn or outright disbelief in sex. Thus, while appearing to claim only that sex is not as central to life as some would make it,

[8] E. R. Dodds, *The Greeks and the Irrational* (Boston: Beacon Press, 1957).
[9] Tom Driver, "On Taking Sex Seriously," *Christianity and Crisis*, Vol. 23, October 14, 1963, pp. 175–79.

Malraux can go on to say that it is the "most animalish" and "the least human part of man." Or Driver, after saying only that sex is as inconsequential as a "frog in the garden," will later admit that sex is "an impersonal, irrational . . . force that turns even the best of men into caricatures of themselves." Driver asks us to laugh at sex, even in marriage, or be humiliated by it. This hardly seems a neutral position. What unites Driver, Gandhi, Augustine, Paul, Plato, and Norman Brown is the unyielding determination to locate human sex somewhere—or anywhere—outside the human self, the authentic "me," that inner core of personhood which makes humanity distinctive. In this one crucial respect, there is no difference between the Christian Fathers' conviction that sex is a "beast in the belly," and Norman Brown's that it is "Christ in me."

What is beneath this experiential dissociation of sex and self? If I am not mistaken, the evidence points to a split experienced between sex and the love-élan, the most intimate, inner principle of the self. When reflective thinkers throughout history have found it impossible to regard human sex as a passion of one's whole being toward personal union and an absolute communion, they have only been looking at the evidence in most lives that the early coalition between Eros and the "human" has broken apart. When man experiences a great contrast between *expectancy* and *event*, ironic or tragic "visions" are the inevitable aftermath. The young lover does not think of his desire for sensual gratification and his desire for spiritual union with the beloved as separate desires; his yearning for bodily communion and his yearning for the Absolute seem one whole élan. This is because the beloved is still for him a source of absolute mystery and being in her infinite-seeming individuality. Much of poetry, the diaries of adolescents, even the accounts by older men of their "first love," illustrate the harmony existing at one time between Eros and the Spirit. It is only a specific set of experiences in life that turns human sex into a ludicrous bit of "fun," or a rebellious "beast below," and turns the atmosphere of the erotic into one of tragedy or irony and self-mockery.

Let us test a hypothesis: that one's view of sex is inevitably determined by one's view of the possibility of love enduring. We will recall that Freud described love ironically as "the overestimation of the sexual object," and that his view of the libido was strikingly subhuman. Unamuno, the Spanish philosopher, writes that his "tragic vision" stemmed from his experience that "love is the child of illusion, the parent of disillusion. Love seeks furiously, through the beloved, something beyond, and since it does not find it, despairs." Predictably, then, we find him describing the sex act as one in which "the souls really hate each other while they embrace." The contrast, as with Freud's ardent love letters and the "realism" of his metapsychology, is one of *expectancy and event*. Christians, too, tend to be shorn of their ardent incarnationalism about this world when it comes to human love, where they grow a bit cynical or, if they prefer, adventist. This is easily illustrated in the work of C. S. Lewis and Chesterton, Barth and Gilson. Chesterton's normal tendency to lacquer over his morbidity with shocking paradoxes of optimism is laid aside when, giving advice to young writers, he declares that "if the novelist wishes to move from romance to marriage, he had best prepare the hero's demise in the first chapter." And not surprisingly, Chesterton rarely saw sex as anything but *lust*, a selfish thirst for epidermal gratification, as one of his famous remarks against the progaganda for contraception illustrated: this movement "of lust without life" will die, he predicted. Otto Piper, the Protestant theoretician on sex, declares unhesitatingly that "there can be no lasting satisfaction in sex or love, despite their promise; there is a divine curse upon them both." And Karl Rahner will warn that "human love must come soberly to terms with the limitations of the beloved," while he defines chastity—and with it, human sex—as the renunciation of the "use of one's power of *generation*" (my italics). Perhaps the most succinct expression of man's disillusionment in sex-and-love is Shakespeare's phrase, "past reason hunted becomes past reason hated." Or as Oscar Wilde summed it up, "the only difference between a caprice and a lifelong passion is that the caprice lasts a little longer." These examples, of course, are selected and cannot fulfill the hypothesis. But I have not yet found, among men like Buber, Dewey, Husserl, Berdyaev, Santayana, Nietzsche,

Camus, Claudel, Mauriac, Beckett, Brecht, Barth, Cézanne, Gilson, Freud, Rimbaud, and many others, any evidence other than that one's view of *sex and the self* can be predicted by the degree of one's real or imagined disappointment in romantic love. Woman, love, and sex, we are continually told, are "promises" that are never kept.

Jeannière's view of woman—one of the weather vanes of one's view of sexuality and love—is essentially personal, as we have seen, and represents a decided advance for Christian theology. He sees man-woman love as a human necessity and as perfectible dynamic relation. But does it endure only in terms of a basically uncritical commitment to the other, for the sake of the child and society? While Jeannière's position here seems to remain ambiguous, he clearly takes several important steps toward a genuine personalist conception of sexual love. Besides, his thought is eminently worth our study for the classic tension it reveals in human thought on this intimate level where memory and ideals may clash.

Jeannière's most important single contribution to the discussion of sex comes, as was mentioned before, in his constant effort to resist the temptation to define sexuality in any way apart from the dynamic history of the couple's relation, "which cannot be described once and for all." He can even wonder whether individuals would possess sexuality if they were kept totally apart from sexual encounter. He notes how man absorbs animal sexuality into his language during childhood, and that afterward this level can never be sifted out for analysis. (Yet he will also say that sexuality remains always prelinguistic, and that "Eros is not logos.") Jeannière goes on, as some Protestant theologians such as D. S. Bailey have done recently, to admonish the Christian tradition for desexualizing man as soon as he is talked of as made in God's image, as if there were no way of speaking of the Trinity's inner life as "sexy." But it is by urging again and again that sex is what man becomes that Jeannière's work is most fruitful and promising, both as psychology and as theological anthropology.

Jeannière's view of sex is personalist in two ways: as regards the unity of human nature, and as regard the effects of sex on man's identity. First, he sees our human sex as both "an aura and a dynamism, all-encompassing factor and source" of our human life. Animal sex was rooted in the biological and aimed at reproduction; human sex is psychological and "now largely transcends this reproductive purpose." Jeannière clearly wishes to escape the charges against past Catholic thinking on sex; he assures us that the evolutionary process has not simply left us half beast and half angel. "There is a unity of human nature . . . the unity of a mobile genesis." And even pure animal sexuality is not a mere biological "need," suggesting that Jeannière might believe that the higher affective and intellectual horizons of human life were prepared for during the vital and biological levels, and that one way to trace the evolution of man would be to follow the development of sexual love. In a slap as past theology, Jeannière notes that in earlier quarrels over evolution, many religious people who were most anxious to demarcate the human from the animal sphere did nevertheless "retain strange views of strict continuity in all that pertains to sexuality." (It is only half a century since one of the leading Catholic moral theology texts, by Noldin, stopped calling the sexual act, even in marriage, "a thing filthy in itself.") Like Merleau-Ponhty, Jeannière wants to assert that the human level has not merely repeated but restructured what went before. For him, the "human level is the birth of an entirely new spiritual world, and is of such importance that the very nature from which it arises is laid open to question." If it is true that the *human* sexual encounter was "invented by man," it is nevertheless true also that the sexual encounter "invented man." Sex thus appears integrally interwoven with human nature.

Beyond this, sexuality is of critical importance in establishing one's identity before the world and before one's self. Echoing much of recent Continental philosophic thought, Jeannière affirms that "my body is my being-in-the-world," and that "it is primarily through my corporeal condition and my sex that I am in the world and for others." He argues that the experience of sex is nothing else than the experience of "transsubjectivity, the basis of all interdependence." And like the man-woman relation in history, the body is a mobile genesis and defies objectification. "The body is not a reality definable once and for all; it escapes as much as does

the mind from the conceptual net in which men try to trap it."
⟨By revealing interpersonal dependence, sex is also man's fundamental guarantee of self-transcendence; his existence is never a
blind alley. He will go a step further and say that, from much of
the evidence, the "only love worth living" is a "full love," apparently referring to love sexually consummated.⟩ (This would echo
Teilhard, who wrote, "At what moment do lovers come into the
most complete possession of themselves, if not when they say they
are lost in each other?"[10] Jeannière calls the sexual-other "the
indispensable developer of one's own ego," and at the conclusion
he writes, ⟨"the genesis of a person, in his totality, requires knowledge (of the other) and recognition (by the other); the person
becomes such only at the interior of a personal relation. . . . Man
becomes man only in the face of an absolute, personal other.⟩"
A quote from Marx, finally, would seem to remove all doubt as to
whether Jeannière is moving in a personalist direction concerning
sex. For Marx, whom he cites, the sex relation "reveals the extent
to which the *human* essence in [man] has become a *natural* essence, the extent to which his *human nature* has come to be *nature
to him*. In this relation is revealed, too, the extent to which man's
need has become a *human need*, the extent to which, therefore,
the *other* person as a person has become for him a need, the extent
to which he is, in his individual existence, at the same time a
social being." The difficulties of interpreting such a text in platonic
and cerebral terms are obvious, but, as a celibate, this seems Jeannière's real task: to retain the man-woman relation; but in the
framework of a kind of spiritual marriage.

For there are signs that Jeannière is uncomfortable with the
personalist conception of sex. Showing the influence perhaps of
French rationalism, he makes a passing yet telling forecast of
future evolution as "a gigantic mutation of the mind," rather
than, for example, as a deepened emotional life. The goal of sexual anthropology is viewed in another passage as "synthesizing
the gestures of love in a *controlled* future development" (my
italics). It is the word "controlled," with the heavy implication
of trust in self-governing reason, that would strike many psy-

[10] Pierre Teilhard de Chardin, *The Phenomenon of Man*, p. 265.

chologists as significant. Is logos any more trustworthy as a human faculty than Eros? And in perhaps the most important passage, Jeannière states—after having already said repeatedly that sex cannot be defined and that it is more of an "aura" and "an all-encompassing factor" in human life—that human sex, after all, is a continuation of animal sex precisely insofar "as erotic impulses go," but that human sex is a break with animal sex in that "mind controls the power of sex." In other words, sex remains in man what it was in the animal, only the mind now controls these "erotic impulses."

Readers should note here how this view is out of harmony, not only with much of what Jeannière himself has implied, but also with leading schools of contemporary psychological analysis, such as the "British school" and many of the "existential" analysts. Fairbairn, for example, declares that Eros is really an integral dynamism of the mind, and that it aims, not at pleasure of the senses, but at something more commensurate with its source in the whole person, namely, union with the other person as person. The ego, says Fairbairn, "is essentially libidinal," that is, person-directed, and erotic impulses are the impulses of my being, not toward sensual gratification, but toward a real or hoped-for specific beloved, or as Jeannière said, a mysterious *individual*. Where Jeannière surprisingly sees all eroticism, or impersonal sexual gestures that deny love and the partner as person, as "having to do only with the body" and animal sexuality, Fairbairn sees them in connection with the history of the whole person, regarding them as desperate lunges, by an ego already torn apart under the pressure of various conflicts, at reestablishing some emotional links with the world. And if it is true at one level that, as Jeannière states, "eroticism hides beneath the mask of love," it is even more true that at a deeper level the fragmented self hides beneath the mask, and *language*, of eroticism. In Fairbairn's words, eroticism and perversions, which to the onlooker—and even to the subject—may seem anonymous and mechanical, the result of a blind, obsessive alien instinct, are in fact efforts of the shattered self to "salvage" something—almost anything—"of natural emotional relationships." It is only when one's history of not being authentically

loved as a whole person, and not being able to love wholly, becomes relatively unbearable, that, as Fairbairn states, "the *inherent
libidinal drive towards the object (person)* leads to . . . aberrant
relationships" (my italics). Masturbation, rape, Don Juanism,
sadism, homosexuality, each "is essentially a technique whereby the
individual seeks to provide for himself an object [person] which
he cannot obtain," and which, in his fantasy life, he pretends this
pseudo-erotic object is.

It is important to have made this short digression before turning to take stock of the profoundly negative attitude which Jeannière can sometimes manifest toward Eros and sexual pleasure.
He sees man's sexual pleasure "as emanating from a deep animality," rather than from personal, total communion with this
beloved. The aim of sexual desire is "the immediate satisfaction
of an "organic overcharge," a mere "relief of tension." This is
purely Freudian, though Jeannière had previously promised to
regard sexuality in terms of a "mobile genesis." Instead, he seems
to see all sex as a univocal and static reality, asserting that human
sex does not in any way even "suggest" or "prepare" the two
human persons for the man-woman encounter. He analyzes the
Tristan-Isolde myth, only to find in Tristan a disastrous collapse
of will, a capitulation of his freedom, rather than a "falling" to
the absolute in Isolde or in their relation. Tristan symbolizes
only an inhuman surrender to the "moment" of "sensual pleasure"
and to the "paroxysm of bodily union." It is "men who give
meaning to animal sex," and again, "it is human love that makes
sex its servant." We seem to be back with Augustine and Jerome
and the beast-in-the-belly.

Where Jeannière seems to see sensual pleasure in many passages
as merely an invitation to be inhuman, we may recall, for contrast's sake, what Fairbairn says: "the function of libidinal pleasure is essentially to provide a signpost to the object" or whole
person, whereas "in Freud's conception . . . the object is regarded
as a signpost to pleasure, and the cart is thus placed before the
horse."[11] Freud's (and Jeannière's) impersonal view of desire and

[11] W. R. D. Fairbairn, *Psychoanalytic Studies of the Personality* X, Bibli-
ography, p. 133.

orgasm derives, says Fairbairn, from an a priori "divorce of [libidinal] energy from psychic structure." But if, in fact, such energy were actually found divorced from the psychic structure, if libidinal or sexual desire did flow from some autonomous, biological mechanism, why should we find, as we invariably do, says Fairbairn, the repression of this energy producing the "phenomena of multiple personality, in which the linkage of repressed 'impulses' to a *submerged ego* is beyond question." What is true, according to Fairbairn and others of the influential "object-relation" school, is that man resists sexual repression because these "repressed 'impulses' are inseparable from the ego structure," rather than deriving from an inherently obstinate animal drive, disordered since the "Fall." Sexual drive is not composed of "impulses" but is the *élan* of my whole self.[12]

The explanation of the basic tension in Jeannière must be sought in the rationale for celibacy, for Jeannière is, after all, one who has thought it legitimate to "give up" sexual love.[13] Christian moral theology long ago absorbed an ancient natural-law tradition which held, rightly, that under normal conditions it is immoral deliberately and systematically to destroy or mutilate anything in yourself pertaining to your essential humanity. As an American theologian, Paul Quay, has written, "One cannot make oneself defective without the radical disorder of freely choosing to be other than one is made to be." J. Fuchs, the German Jesuit and one of the leading *periti* at the Vatican Council, has put the same idea this way: "As sexuality shows, it could be that a creature . . . has still another finality than that which is directly expressed in the biological nature of this creature. Finalities and orders which the spiritual and personal nature of man manifest are all obligatory, because they belong to the 'being' and not to the 'having' of the human person." Only if sex is something I *have*, and is not something I *am*, can celibacy be a legitimate vocation.

---

12 Dan Sullivan, "Sex and the Person," *Commonweal*, July 22, 1966, pp. 460–64.

13 Dan Sullivan, "Celibacy and the Contraception Debate," in *The National Catholic Reporter*, June 29, 1966; "A History of Catholic Thinking on Contraception," in *What Modern Catholics Think About Birth Control*, W. Birmingham, ed. (New York: New American Library, 1964), pp. 28–72.

The procreative motif in Catholic theology, repeated warnings about "unbridled lust" that evoke images of a raging beast below, the emphasis on woman as "mother" and "heart of the home," all these strands of Catholic thought, may well have as their unconscious source the need of the celibate to deny that his sexuality represents an integrally personal passion.

Jeannière makes express reference to the need he feels to defend celibacy. He sees its justification as a search for "modes of intimacy beyond eroticism" and for "concrete but universal forms of love." The reduction of sexual desire and pleasure to "eroticism," and of eroticism to an animal instinct, serves his defense of celibacy by making room for the possibility of a higher relation than the sexual. Indeed, Jeannière at times seems to place human sex ontologically apart from man as man. Sex posits itself to *me* for the sake of the species, and for me as an individual. "This is the exact point where I can affirm the strength of *my own autonomous and personal position,* or where I can renounce and lose myself in a nature that is mine but outside myself" (p. 75—my italics). And further on, "the sexed body becomes an element of personal destiny only to the extent and in the mode it is accepted and assumed" (p. 111). There would seem to remain an unresolved tension between these statements and Jeannière's view of sex as a mobile genesis coextensive with human genesis, or as an aura and all-encompassing factor as well as source of the human being.

This book, then, represents a sincere and telling attempt to lift Catholic thought above its historic dualism and free it of contamination by pre-Christian biologistic views of sexual love and marriage. A tension remains, to emerge in Jeannière's defense of celibacy. But even Teilhard de Chardin has a highly abstract and basically infrapersonal view of woman. Abel Jeannière is perhaps the first Christian theologian, at least of Catholic persuasion, to opt firmly on the side of woman-as-a-person. He insistently defines the person as being-for-the-other. With these two major steps, joined to his repeated insistence that sexuality is to be studied only in terms of a dynamic man-woman encounter, he has made a truly important advance in the elaboration of theological anthropology. He has clarified its goal: to see and present marriage not in the static cyclic terms of a finished reality, but in the inherently dynamic idealism of the Incarnation. Jeannière's view of woman is wholly and dynamically human; among Christian writers, it is a true landmark in the efforts to evolve a more cogent theology of marriage.

DAN SULLIVAN

CONTENTS

27

The Anthropology of Sex

INTRODUCTION

The words *masculine* and *feminine* assuredly have a meaning. Is it a precise meaning, and the same in every country? Try to give them a significance without falling into dubious banality or sociological approximation! Chance led me to formulate my curiosity more precisely when, substituting for another professor, I had to give a course at the Institute of Social Studies (the Catholic Institute of Paris) and found myself confronted by the vagueness of the too familiar, further obscured by an immense and very disparate literature on the subject. The tone of this book is perhaps too didactic, because it is the résumé of a course; it is at any rate an attempt to see things clearly by eliminating as many preconceived judgments as possible. Radical questions are asked at the start, for nothing is less certain than what is well known. Neither is anything more important than love, which together with death is one of the phenomena that affect the totality of the human being. The anxiety caused by our thoughts of death results from the radical isolation to which we are driven; love, on the contrary, is the privileged ground for our encounter with another as a human being. In this encounter and this union what is it, then, to be a man and to be a woman? What are the male and the female beyond and within this meeting? For the sexuality underlying it extends past it on all sides.

The sexuality which is present at the beginning of every human life, both as source and as all-encompassing entity, permeates that life for its whole duration. As the result of evolution, it has repercussions at all levels of humanity and beyond the social to the spiritual. In no way can it be circumscribed so as to fix it as a definable object of study. Nor, owing to its fundamental character, can sexuality be taken as a principle or simple line of explanation; we cannot follow it in its harmonious growth, like a seed whose shoots rise at the various stages of human life. The frequent method of progressing from the biological to the psychological, then from the psycho-sociological to the spiritual and to love, follows only an artificial course. No order has been pursued that could, in any terms, be called that of sexuality; and there will certainly be found at its every level the most diverse transpositions, yet in each it manifests itself as an aura and a dynamism—as an all-encompassing factor and as source.

The rational path we shall try to trace across the thousand forms of sexuality and the interpretations to which they give rise calls for supplementary explanation, and its bias should be admitted. The path starts from a point where sexuality has already found meaning: in the encounter of man and woman and their confrontation. Our research, whether uniting or contrasting them, does not separate sexuality from love. We start from a given meaning and look for the underlying foundations; start, not with definitions, but from the very question that arises. The love that binds two beings in a union of flesh and spirit enables sexuality to pass beyond shame and modesty, beyond erotic play, and beyond the pleasure that is enhanced by tenderness. But the object of this study is still sexuality, not love. Sexuality is itself the source of ambiguity; in it a voice rising from the species intermingles and clashes—a voice from primeval origins underlying and cutting across the childish language and human speech that organize the history of sex.

Human sexuality unfolds in the family, a closed circle, and here we raise our questions. This study is certainly not an inquiry into the family values with which it occasionally deals, but a radical investigation into the genesis and growth of human sexuality. Why is a human being either man or woman, masculine or feminine? What is the meaning? And along what lines has sexuality developed?

The family is the first social reality that allows us to proceed from a concrete whole—self-existent, proximate, and visible—to the individuals who are defined by that whole. Comparisons with the mating of animals do not allow us to reach the level of an explanation but merely throw light on conditioning factors. The whole, says Hegel, appears only as a "substance of the spirit." To study the family means to study, not individuals living side by side, but a dynamic whole in which the relations between persons form those persons, even their individuality. "The family, as the immediate substantiality of mind, is specifically characterized by love, which is mind's feeling of its own unity. Hence in a family one's frame of mind is to have consciousness of one's individuality within this unity as the absolute essence of self, with the result that one is in it not as an independent person but as a member."[1]

What are the anthropological foundations of family life? The foundations of a human reality can only be human. "Marriage is sometimes said to be grounded not in natural rights but simply in instinctive sexual impulses; or again it is treated as a contract with an arbitrary basis. External arguments in support of monogamy have been drawn from physical considerations such as the number of men and women. Dark feelings of repulsion are advanced as the sole ground for prohibiting consanguineous marriage. The basis of all these views is in general . . . the lack of the concept of rationality and freedom."[2]

After Hegel, Marx who criticizes him—that is to say, who discerningly follows his youthful steps—was to say that man's relation to woman is the most "natural" in the sense that it reveals the level of humanity reached in social life and shows the extent to which "the other person, as a person, has become for him a need."[3]

What path leads from the need, which impels the race to reproduce itself by the multiplication of individuals, to man's preference for his own species? What roles does sexuality play in this progression? Where does the dialectical reversal take place that puts sexuality at the service of love and permits it to unfold beyond itself in a human world not of its making?

Many of those who consider the effective evolutionary passage from the biological to the social, and from animal to man, not as a simple development but as a change of sphere, retain strange views of strict continuity in all that pertains to sexuality. Yet sexual

[1] G. W. F. Hegel, *Philosophy of Right*, T. M. Knox, trans. (Oxford: Clarendon Press, 1953), § 158, p. 110.
[2] *Ibid.*, § 168, R, p. 115.
[3] Karl Marx, *Economic and Philosophic Manuscripts of 1844*, Martin Milligan, trans. (New York: International Pubilshers, 1964), p. 134.

need reaches well beyond the call to procreation, not only in affectivity but further, and into the most abstract intellectual meditations. What is the meaning of the personal dimension of sexuality? What is its link with the pursuit of animal impulses? What is the play of sexual differentiation on the human level? What is the significance of the confrontation of man and woman; is it possible to discern in it aspects of dialogue and conflict?

I have been struck by the important implications of the texts, and have been curious about the possibilities of expansion which one surmises in reading the short passages that Hegel and Marx devote to the man-woman relationship as a fundamental dialectic. Both of them give preferential treatment, and Marx a quasi-exclusive treatment, to the developments of the master-slave dialectic in labor and the struggle of classes. How can this dialectic of disjunction account for the aspiration toward unity which, despite everything, is discernible amid the conflicts, the antagonisms, and the greater acuteness of personal and collective awareness? The studies of Père G. Fessard have drawn my attention to the intervening role of the two dialectics, one of disjunction, the other of union. The man-woman dialectic is, in fact, a dialectic of union, in reverse, yet just as fundamental as the master-slave dialectic. It is the intervening role of these two dialectics that produces the historical entity that we are today.[4]

But while it is important to uncover these intervening roles in the genesis of society as Père Fessard has done,[5] should not an understanding of the man-woman dialectical relationship be based on an understanding of sexuality? Before all history and underlying the course of history, at every moment and always necessary for man as man, there is the fundamental relationship of the sexes. I was surprised to note that the analyses of the man-woman relationship, as psychologists, sociologists, and philosophers deal with it from their various viewpoints, most often put this foundation itself between parentheses, so to speak, precisely because it is a

[4] Cf. A. Jeannière, "Le Triple Dialectique de l'Histoire," introduction to the work of Père G. Fessard, *Archives de Philosophie* (April–June 1961), pp. 242–59.

[5] G. Fessard, "Le Mystère de la société. Recherches sur le sens de l'Histoire," *Recherches de Science religieuse*, Nos. 1 and 2, 1948.

foundation. Or they write in the perspective of the master-slave dialectic, which at least permits them to place themselves in a social life that is in the process of becoming, and to analyze the relationship of man and woman as a conflict of the sexes. A justifiable view, but perhaps partial. Or they sum up behavior which would be difficult to define and which perhaps does not belong to the same dimension of social life. Or, more frequently, they are satisfied to connect, more or less artificially, empirical views which they consider wise with moral principles that cannot always be distinguished from traditions. For example, they aim at a complementarity of individuals, viewed abstractly as already existing in some sort of vacuum. Finally, sociological upheavals make evident the first signs of the collapse of numerous categories whose solidity had been affirmed too soon. Is it too soon to discern the direction of these shifting movements?

An article by Erwin Metzcke gave me a clearer insight into my at times disappointing, at others enlightening reading of a vast body of literature in which certain important works stand out. I have tried to arrange my ideas by taking as guide the progressive disclosure of the fundamental requirements of the encounter between man and woman. Sometimes I do no longer recall to whom I owe the idea that was the point of departure for one or another of my paragraphs.

This study is an attempt at a rational arrangement, a methodical outline of reflections based on the interpersonal relation of the sexes, one which meets with other reflections and examines them in passing but aims above all else at tracing a succinct line, even cutting across present-day investigations, in order to make a positive contribution to anthropology. Our object is to dispel the mystique of pseudo foundations—biological, psychoanalytical, and sociological—that has gathered around the sexes, and yet to show simultaneously, in the very tension that opposes and unites them, the originality of love and its biological roots, the need for intimacy, and the social factors that condition it. Our purpose is to interpret love beyond the schemas and stereotypes of "natures," in the truth and freedom of personal relationships, in order to reveal the ultimate horizons man may reach.

This study, of course, does not entirely avoid a certain abstractness; its arrangement is logical. A study of love in its concrete genesis in personal and social history, from the psychoanalytical and sociological points of view, still remains to be made. This essay is concerned only with philosophical anthropology and remains on that level. Nor should the reader expect here an exposition or justification of Christian conceptions of love. I do not dismiss attempts at formulating a Christian anthropology, nor the religious ramifications that come from within to aid rational exigencies; neither do I look for them. I refer to them at times, but my aim is different. The question of divorce for example, would no doubt have appeared less controversial in another context. This study is intended simply as a rational analysis, a logical reflection, on the level of a phenomenology of human love.

And yet, my limited project may appear highly ambitious. What matters is that these pages may help some reader to clarify his views, by expressing and putting into order what many already surmise, and by arousing discussion that may lead to progress.

CHAPTER ONE

The Weight of History and Actuality:
The Sexual Question

To write a history of the family would be a gigantic undertaking. Few authors have attempted it since Friedrich Engels' remarkable, ambiguous, and hasty work, forcibly compressed into a system, and—above all else—premature.[1] Only one period and one aspect are pertinent to our subject. To what extent has the family—as it has developed in recent centuries in Europe and particularly France, in a fundamentally patriarchal civilization, as a "natural" way of life—contributed to our quasi-imperative image which continues to dominate the relation between man and woman in their love life or daily life, despite opposition and reappraisal? To what extent has it objectified into "eternal" types the relations actually experienced in a given sort of family belonging to our culture and depending on economic conditions?

BEFORE THE REVOLUTION

We are just beginning to forget the patriarchal period. Before the Revolution the head of the family ruled, and his rule was at "the foundation of national society," in the words of Restif de la Bretonne. No child, no woman would ever become truly adult. Before being anything whatever in society, one was a member and representative of a family. Up to the year 1938, the Civil Code

[1] *The History of Human Marriage* by Edward Westermarck, 3 vols. (5th ed.; London: Macmillan & Co., 1921) is a valuable source of information, but its arrangement is rather arbitrary and its reasoning defective.

reminded woman at the time of marriage that she "owes obedience to her husband." The altered text merely softens the formula: the husband is the head of the family, an institution which the Code does not recognize as an institution; woman is no longer told to obey, but her husband is told to command. "Woman is for man," the Code maintains; and "man for God only," Milton added in *Paradise Lost*. Yet the evolution of customs is increasingly rapid, and this husbands' paradise looks dubious, about to vanish.

In the Middle Ages a certain counterweight came at times from the Church: she requires the consent of both partners. This led to frequent clashes with the head of the family, because the consent of the daughter became indispensable (there were of course many ways to extort consent). Worse yet, the Church allowed marriage without the consent of the parents and well before the age of twenty-one; Shakespeare was to show us in *Romeo and Juliet* what conflicts could ensue.

Only much later, certain moralists tended to make a greater virtue of submission than of freedom. With the development of communes, and especially after the Council of Trent, marriages of interest were to increase in midlle-class society.

In the country, families were large, although it is difficult to find exact statistics. In the middle classes, a family of ten to fifteen children was normal and desirable.[2] Among the revolutionaries, for instance, Carnot was one of fifteen children, Catinat of sixteen, Saint-Just of ten.

Many women died in childbirth, as did Robespierre's mother when she had her fifth child. An estimated forty out of every thousand infants died at birth. The stability of the population (or rather its slow growth) was assured not by wars but by epidemics, famine, and especially infant mortality. Forty-three per cent of the children died before the age of ten. Among the poorer classes many children were abandoned; in Paris at the time of the Revolution one child in ten was a foundling.

Resolutely and invariably, policies and Sunday sermons were

[2] L. Abensour, *La Femme et féminisme avant la Révolution*, (Paris: Leroux, 1923), p. 173. "In the average bourgeoisie, families of ten, twelve, fifteen children were frequently found." Unfortunately the author gives no examples.

populationist. Colbert tried to assure fathers of families with more than ten children of employment and relief from taxation. But this project very quickly appeared too onerous, and was soon dropped.

Aged people were few enough to be venerated, especially when they could lay claim to the honors of the patriarchate. They were the "wise men" who gathered others around them to receive the counsels of experience, counsels valid only insofar as society had in fact undergone no perceptible change since their own youth. They were privileged, survivors, witnesses to eternal rules.

With notable exceptions, woman had no choice save between the religious life and marriage. If she married, she was destined to become the mother of a large family. In the country she was a faded old woman at twenty-five; this was her lot, her destiny, her vocation. She could escape only by "spiritual motherhood" in an active religious order, or by consecrating her virginity in a contemplative order. At any rate, her role was to be good and not beautiful.

In those days, moralists and theologians already had elaborate doctrines of the sacrament of marriage—a situation often aggravated by the fact that these cloistered thinkers were with rare exceptions woman-haters, and held a pessimistic view of marriage. Had not their master, Aristotle, said that the most lascivious females were the woman and the mare, the only two to mate with the male when they were already pregnant![3]

The essential value of marriage was thought to be the family patrimony and the insurance of its perpetuation through generations. The law of primogeniture, which guaranteed this transmittal, had its counterpart in the dowry or marriage portion, the compensation given to younger sons and daughters so that they would renounce their right to the land and the house. Vieille-Michel writes: "The family identified itself with the ancestral patrimony, most often landed estates that assured the subsistence of the family from generation to generation." But, as already noted, only with the rise of the middle classes did "family morals" tend to be identified "with rules relative to the mainten-

[3] Aristotle, *On the generation of Animals*, IV, 773b, 774a. On the development of scholastic thought, see L. Vereecke, "Mariage et sexualité au déclin du moyen âge," *La Vie Spirituelle*, Supplément, No. 57 (2d trimester, 1961), pp. 199 ff.

ance and transmittal of this patrimony."[4] With the institution of marriage, society defended the stability of its economy.

Celibacy was the exception for the eldest male, but could be exacted of the younger son as a sacrifice to the family.[5] Every marriage was a family affair, a question of economy and social order, into which love unfortunately entered sometimes as a complicating factor.

While the role assigned to woman did not permit the organization of a true female society with its own secrets and its own hierarchy such as we note in certain other cultures, segregation of the sexes was imposed in rural society. It prevailed in church, in education—directed for the woman toward household tasks—and in public life, where the café and even the common table of the farm remained gathering places for the men. Segregation in the schools continued throughout the nineteenth century, and there were even "female humanities," since the woman was to be prepared only for her role as mistress of the household.

SURVIVAL OF AGRARIAN MODELS

We shall not retrace the course of history. There was to be a mixture of the influences of Malthus, individualism, Marxist ideas, and the somewhat primitive views of the French socialists.

With the coming of industry, the rise of the middle class is linked with the great individualistic thrust of liberalism. From the baptismal register one passed to the civil record office, which became obligatory. Stability was more and more assured on new

4 Andrée Vieille-Michel, "Famille, Société industrielle et Démocratie," *Esprit* (November 1960), p. 1762. Adrienne Sahuqué wrote at the conclusion of her book, *Les Dogmes sexuels* (Paris: F. Alcan, 1932), p. 372: "One might say that obsession with inheritance, the vehicle of law, has dominated from time immemorial the entire notion of heredity and sexuality, this notion being always conceived, desired, and discussed as a certain mode of economic and juridical transmittal." Adrienne Sahuqué developed her point of view with arguments which make her in some ways a precursor of Simone de Beauvoir.

5 Celibacy of the eldest son was a kind of failure of the system; but for the younger sons celibacy "could be understood as a natural sacrifice of the individual to the collective interest." P. Bourdieu, "Célibat et Condition paysanne," *Études rurales*, Nos. 5–6 (1962), p. 59.

political bases. Interest in agriculture no longer predominated and was beginning to wane. Ideologies began to clash.

With this affirmation of the individual, romantic love could appear and passion be glorified. The democratization of passion and romantic love are at the opposite pole from courtly love. The humanism evinced in courtly love could appear only within a strong feudal structure—a version of that structure by which one could pass beyond it. The vassal lover was ennobled by the love of the sovereign lady, whom he sometimes called by the masculine *mi doms*, my lord. We must not forget the essential trait of courtly love: it was an aristocratic exaltation of adultery; in the days of the troubadours it did not seem altogether normal for a man to be in love with his wife. Love could certainly come into being in the home, but marriage was not the outcome of a great passion. Romantic love abolished the distance between the lady and her lover; it was above all a proclamation of the unlimited rights of the individual.

At the beginning of the industrial era, the middle-class family ceased to be large. The link between living standard and number of children became the reverse of what it had been for the rural family; the child was a liability, no longer an asset. The family was further marked by puritanism, the cult of individual virtue, and concern to keep up social appearances. Antagonism between the middle-class family and the working-class family also began at that time.

Still, the rural type of family survived and was still exalted as the Christian ideal. The rural family, with its diversified roles of husband and wife, continued to inspire most of the edifying discourses on marriage and family. This survival of images and structures in a different context is a familiar sociological phenomenon.

But then especially, the ancient family conceived not only as "the unit of production and consumption,"[6] but as the fundamental cell from which all social relationships grew and were organized, represented much more a mental image rather than a "natural" way of life. At that time, evolution tended to compensate social mutations by greater conceptual systemization.

[6] Vieille-Michel, *op. cit.*, p. 1756.

Raymond Deniel rightly stresses the capital role played in Catholic and conservative circles by the views of the traditionalist authors Joseph de Maistre and especially Louis de Bonald.

> The latter felt it necessary systematically to justify conditions as lived under the *ancien régime*, which the French Revolution, by instituting divorce and upgrading the individual, had placed in deadly danger. To prevent them from being constantly questioned, in other words to bar them from any evolution judged to be dangerous, he aimed at establishing these conditions as the natural state of things. With him, however, the natural state of society is the perfection it acquires at the end of a long process starting with the natural state, and this perfection is revealed and willed by God. French society had reached this point before the Revolution.[7]

The country was a hierarchy of families in which the analogy in roles influenced the various levels of civic life. The king was father of the state, as the father was in charge of the family; both exercised paternal authority in the likeness of and dependence on the divine fatherhood over the world. And the standing of the family was clearly linked to the transmittal of the hereditary patrimony on which nobility was based.

"Deeply shaken and challenged by the French Revolution, the Church of France in the nineteenth century easily adopted a system based on natural and providential laws, placing the family and religion in first rank, justifying her own mistrust of urban civilization and of republican institutions."[8] The middle class found itself at ease in the proclamation of "natural" laws that justified its economic conceptions, especially because these laws gave the head of the family the power to enlarge its capital by controling family alliances.

Before systemization accentuated the break with real life, a human equilibrium had become established in the rural family. The transplantation of that family into urban life was to upset the balance. Like the valiant woman of the Bible, the mother

[7] Raymond Deniel, "Femmes dans la ville," *Revue de l'Action Populaire* (March 1964), p. 288.
[8] *Ibid.*, p. 283.

directed the economy of the large household. Of this household, she was both the symbol and the provider. The husband could not be punished for adultery committed outside the home; woman could be punished for it, because she carried the home with her. Mediatrix between nature and culture, she gave birth, fed, and educated the whole man; linked to the animal world by her role in generation, linked even to the monthly cycles in her body, in mysterious harmony with the fertility of the sustaining soil; she was the mother, and her role as educator had deep roots in these realities of the flesh. In her, maternal instinct had grown into a vocation for motherhood. Mediatrix between groups separated by distance in space and by generations in time, she communicated life; through woman, alliances were made between families as between states.

Thus upon her devolved a whole social role which was often broadening. This role was considered natural and willed by God in a world where God, master of "nature," ruled the cycles and seasons. He rewarded or punished through nature. He was master of hail and thunder, sun and rain. All this would change when winegrowers came to place greater trust in the anti-hail cannon than the religious procession, when meteorological satellites were launched, when women found hormones more effective than pilgrimages.

In that organized universe, woman was in her place willed by God. She was to find her greatness in the development of her femininity. Since society seemed basically unchangeable, the place of woman was established in nature and in substance. There was a female nature, a female psychology, a female temperament, just as there are female bodies and organs. But all this "nature" could develop into real or sublimated motherhood. How many tributes have been laid on the altar of the Mother and the Eternal Feminine!

It now has become clear that agrarian "nature" is fading into the past, and that the current crises and transformations in agriculture are its last convulsions. Yet "our villages still retain a form whose content, life and meaning have disappeared: the cemetery and the church, cells of space, centers of time, regulators of rhythms and cycles. An organization and a symbolism about to disappear have left visible traces which are becoming less and less legible to modern eyes."[9]

WOMAN'S SUBJECTION TO SERVITUDE

This "natural" status was highly convenient to "the male of the species," yet in the middle-class family it became more and more difficult to defend. Molière's Chrysale already saw the emancipation of woman as a threat to his doublets and breeches. To tell the truth, many masculine recriminations did not rise above this level of needs. Who will darn the socks and put the soup on the stove? Fortunately, technology has come to the aid of the woman: she no longer repairs socks, and a factory makes and packages the soup.

Were women really slaves? In any case they felt like slaves, particularly when rural culture entered the industrial era, keeping as many as possible of its old habits and stereotypes. The equilibrium of an agrarian civilization could not be transposed into an industrial world. The attempted transposition was to lead to slavery which, like every form of slavery, would find its apologists. Aristotle had said that slavery was necessary for mankind to reach its highest fulfillment in the person of certain of its representatives. The true man should not be crushed by the struggle with nature for the satisfaction of his needs. Before slavery could be abolished, he said, shuttles would have to work themselves. He thought he was putting off the abolition of slavery forever. As it happens, woman's emancipation began to make progress precisely at the time when shuttles began to run by themselves.

We do not intend here to analyze the positions taken by thinkers and theologians, but rather to point out the connection between a certain view of woman and a culture.

Our picture of the family before the Revolution would be incomplete without a look at the opinions of the philosophers of the Enlightenment. It is enough to reread Book V of Rousseau's *Emile*, entitled "Sophie, or Woman."

[9] Henri Lefebvre, *Introduction à la modernité* (Paris: Editions de Minuit, 1962), p. 154.

Of the two sexes, J. J. Rousseau says, "man should be strong and active, woman weak and passive. . . . Woman is made to please and to be in subjection to man."[10]

"A woman's education must be planned in relation to man. To be pleasing in his sight, to win his respect and love, to train him in childhood, to tend him in manhood, to counsel and console, to make his life pleasant and happy, these are the duties of woman for all time, and this is what she should be taught while she is young."[11]

"As a woman's conduct is controlled by public opinion, so is her religion ruled by authority. The daughter should follow her mother's religion, the wife her husband's. Were that religion false, the docility which leads mother and daughter to submit to nature's laws would blot out the sin of error in the sight of God. Unable to judge for themselves, they should accept the judgment of father and husband as that of the Church."[12]

And here is Rousseau's reference to the inevitable vocation to motherhood: "Women, you say, are not always bearing children. Granted; yet that is their proper business."[13]

We have here still another allusion to the proper business of nature, which often means no more than the writer's own preference. Rousseau has at least the twofold merit of frankness and of speaking without a mythology. Yet it seems to me that logically his ideal would be the harem.

The article on "Woman" in Diderot's *Encyclopédie* affirms the specific differences between the sexes, but apparently with greater reservation: "Women differ from men in heart and mind no less than in stature and shape, yet their natural dispositions are modified in so many ways by education, their souls are so veiled by that secretiveness which seems for them an imperative of their state, the exceptions are so great and so confused with generalities, that any further observations only tend to obscure the conclusions to

---

10 *Emile*, Barbara Foxley trans., "Everyman's Library," No. 518 (London: J. M. Dent & Sons; New York: E. P. Dutton & Co., 1948), p. 322.

11 *Ibid.*, p. 328.

12 *Ibid.*, p. 340.

13 *Ibid.*, p. 325.

be drawn."[14] These remarks are fair, but they are unfortunately followed by an example of woman's capriciousness.[15]

"Unable to judge for themselves"—such is the refrain down through history. St. Thomas, who sees woman as an inferior being, as a "defective male," here joins hands with the philosophers of the Enlightenment. A woman is a man minus certain qualities, mainly physical. One could easily compile a sort of "bestiary" made up of quotations from the philosophers. "Cats, that is what women are, cats or birds. Or, if everything goes well, they are cows," wrote Friedrich Nietzsche. Proudhon says: "The woman is halfway between man and ape," agreeing with St. Thomas when he wrote: "If we look at nature in particular individuals, woman is something defective, something imperfect."[16]

The trouble lies here. St. Thomas joins hands with Jean Jacques Rousseau, the Middle Ages with the middle-class revolution; all that has changed are the modes and conceptions of woman's inferiority. In the nineteenth century Proudhon joined with Louis de Bonald and, though woman's condition has begun to change, many today still retain an opinion similar to that frankly set forth by Montherlant in *Les Jeunes Filles*: "The man who gets married always makes a gift to the woman, because she has need of marriage and he does not. . . . Woman is made for man, and man is made for life." Coming at the end of a declaration of individualism, is the word life more apposite here than the word God?

Are we to conclude that the relation of the sexes is a social struggle of the master-slave type? Does the man-woman relation concern the human subject, as a subject, other than as a challenge similar to the class struggle? What is the meaning today of the

[14] Vol. XIII, p. 931.
[15] Montesquieu has moreover a biological explanation for this capriciousness: "The difference between the sexes also leads to a diversity in minds. The revolution which takes place periodically in women has a very broad effect. It even assails the mind. We know that it is caused by a fullness which increases continuously for around one month; after this the great quantity of blood which has collected forces its passage outside. Now, since each day this quantity changes within them, the moods and dispositions of women also change." Charles de Montesquieu "Essai sur les causes qui peuvent affecter les espirits et les caractères," *Oeuvres complètes* (Paris: Éditions du Seuil, 1964), p. 488.
[16] *Sum. Theol.*, Ia, q. 92, ad 1.

movement for woman's emancipation? Must we say with Henri Lefebvre: "Nevertheless, the battle of the sexes continues. We have yet to see the disappearance of the old antagonism between manhood and womanhood living side by side as rival entities and in defiance of each other"?[17]

As to the agrarian myths, woman today either smiles or is irritated by them; sometimes she will go along with them, though without conviction. These myths are hackneyed and mumified, yet everybody uses language which suggests their survival. No longer living truths, these myths still persist. Yet is the woman always a mediatrix, and between what nature and what culture? What value has the symbolism of cycles and its various versions, those references as irritating as gnats to evanescent "femininity," which do nothing to penetrate to the mystery of sex?

Despite the most diverse circumstances, and systems and ideologies notwithstanding, love remains possible—the love which is the key word of our inquiry and to which a Greek poet, the pseudo Phocydides, paid tribute a century before Plato in these words: "Nothing so warms the heart, nothing is so wonderful as two spouses living to old age, and loving one another with nothing ever to divide them."

NEW PERSPECTIVES: SOCIAL EVOLUTION, TECHNICAL AND BIOLOGICAL ADVANCES

Woman's entry into public life is stressed by John XXIII in *Pacem in Terris* as one of the characteristics of the present, a development with tremendous and unforeseeable consequences. That woman has reached adult status is already manifest in the more frequent and pressing civic, professional, and social responsibilities she claims.[18]

Will a change now take place in woman's ambiguous and narrow role in history?[19] Traditional images, though more and more inadequate, persist and still dominate.

However, social evolution, technical and biological progress,

---

[17] Lefebvre, *op. cit.*, p. 156.
[18] *Pacem in Terris* (Glen Rock, N.J.: Paulist Press, 1963), par. 41, p. 17.
[19] Cf. Olga Wormser, *Les femmes dans l'Histoire* (Paris: Correa, 1952).

and a new viewpoint on the problems of sex and reproduction are converging. All these profundly modify the social and conceptual complex surrounding the man-woman relation.

As early as 1944 a physician triumphantly announced before the British Society of Forensic Medicine: "We have reached the stage where we need no longer leave births to the chance of amorous impulses; we now have before us a biological phenomenon of the same order as the transplantation of microbe colonies. At least on the part of the male contribution, semination can be selective." (He did not refer to the criteria of this selection.) The deciphering of the genetic code today opens other possibilities more difficult to exploit immediately but of far greater long-range importance.

Even apart from the social, philosophical, and moral principles involved in human experimentation,[20] eugenics poses a multiple problem with social aspects that are already evident. And if ectogenesis is still a remote possibility, individual genetic charts, charts of our molecular cells, can be expected in the near future. What will happen when the biologist's indications are combined with psychological orientation before marriage—when lovers can no longer choose to make the game of love a game of chance?

Contemporary literature, scientific or fictional, tends more and more to separate the sexual act from procreation and to destroy family ties once considered essential. If the sperm become interchangeable through artificial insemination, will the man-woman relation take a secondary place in marriage? Will it be replaced by the relation between child and mother, or by some other? If so, what will form the basis of the intimate relation in the conjugal community? Or is this community itself destined to disappear?

Certain sociologists tend even now to consider love a negligible factor in sexual behavior; examples are Alfred C. Kinsey and his colleagues, or Clellan S. Ford and Frank A. Beach.[21] Their sexology

[20] Cf. "Mutation de l'homme," special number of *Revue de l'Action Populaire* (November 1962).

[21] Alfred E. Kinsey and Others, *Sexual Behavior in the Human Male* (Philadelphia: W. B. Saunders Co., 1948). Also Alfred E. Kinsey and Paul Gebhard, *Sexual Behavior in the Human Female* (Philadelphia: W. B. Saunders Co., 1953). Clellan S. Ford and Frank A. Beach, *Patterns in Sexual Behavior* (New York: Harper & Brothers, 1951).

aims to analyze sexual behavior in men and animals by trying to determine the influence of social structures. Behavior is defined as the pattern of sexual acts—but, in the final analysis, of what acts? What we are given is a description of various modes of rut, with statistics of their frequency and of various other ways of arriving at an orgasm. Does this even begin to deal realistically with human sexuality? The boldness of this seeming objectivity actually favors sexual improvisation and anarchy.

Economists study the family almost exclusively as a consumer of goods and producer of children. They would determine the size of families in keeping with optimum economic development. Their criteria are primarily related to policies of full employment, investment possibilities, and the growth of the national income. For them, family policy is an element of economic policy, but here the interest is in long-range planning, and in the possibilities and prospects of control even at the family level. All this could be facilitated by man's recent mastery, certain to be confirmed, of biological mechanisms and fecundity. The tendency is to exclude all spontaneity or empiricism from married intimacy.

This approach could lead to a liberation of the sexual instinct at the individual level, for the reason or under the pretext that it will no longer have social repercussions. Even more, it would appear natural that people should seek various modes of liberating the sex impulse, in order to make up for the controls of planning.

In this light, can the family subsist other than as an element of something larger, namely sexuality? Conjugal life is a way of satisfying the sexual drives which involves a number of social consequences. There are a multitude of other ways of satisfying this need which do not have the same inconveniences, but neither do they have the same advantages.

But on the whole, social pressures are balanced in a double tendency: to plan procreation by various methods at the social level, and to seek compensation by sexual anarchy at the individual level.

QUESTIONS AND METHODS

With all these investigations and propositions, with all these new social complexes, a number of questions regarding sexual life remain to be answered.

How can we describe a sexuality that is truly and fully human? Is it certain that a comparison with animal life is the only approach, the best, or even valid at all? Are sociological observations sufficient to establish a direction in the rapid movement of our cultures? Still more fundamental, what defines man and woman, not merely male and female, as two sexual beings?

If it were possible not to define or limit but rather to point out, to proclaim, even perhaps to present human sexuality as desirable—along what line, then, would such sexuality have the greatest chance of development? Over and above the multiple ways of satisfying a need, how can the optimum development of human sexuality be attained?

Alfred Kinsey, for one, answers none of these questions. He tells us what is most frequent—but frequency is not a norm; it is especially not a sign of success. Why, after all, should one not say with André Gide: "You and I, Nicodème, we are with the small number of the elect"? Nor can we start with the hypothesis that nothing related to sexuality is of importance in the search for greater human self-fulfillment. Certain extraordinarily successful examples might lead us rather to the contrary assumption, that only a great love makes life worth living.

Moreover, the sexual act is not a thing, though it may of course be treated as such. It might even be asked to what extent it can be considered an object of positive science.[22] The Kinsey report defines sexuality as "a normal biological function, acceptable under any form it may assume." This leads to the enumeration and classification of data arbitrarily selected or defined; but what among these data pertains to sexuality and what does not? Further, the investigator has to classify behavior that cannot be observed; he works only with the reinterpretation of sexual behavior, the double reinterpretation by himself and by the person interviewed.

[22] G. Bataille, "Le Rapport Kinsey," *Critique* (August 1948).

No doubt the person interviewed ordinarily gives a frank answer much more often than chronic critics might imagine, but "at best, he may be asked how many times he has made love with such and such a woman, but he is not asked if he loves her or loves someone else."[23]

The fact is that sexuality escapes the data that sociologists ordinarily delight in handling. Sexuality is pretechnical and does not involve contact with nature and its transformations, or the world of work, at least not unless it is considered only in relation to the techniques of the body, or unless there is a question of the adjustment of sexual organs or of preventive measures. If marriage is an institution, sexuality is just the opposite, a force which is in opposition to everything determined and defined by society. It does not lend itself to observable behavior because—and this is graver still—it does not enter the field of the language and figures used to reinterpret it. As Paul Ricœur writes: "It is Eros and not Logos. It is radically impossible to incorporate it into the element of Logos."[24]

When we make sexuality an object of science, do we not annihilate it, reduce it to the commonplace and insignificant? To call it a biological function as normal as eating or urinating deprives it of all proper meaning. The vulgarization of the behavior involved affects freedom; it depersonalizes it. What could become at least affective engagement is immediately lost in anonymity. The sexual encounter becomes easy but no longer has meaning.

Even on the animal plane sexuality cannot be confused with simple need; this is what prevents us from considering the animal as simply a thing, as G. Bataille, following Hegel, emphasizes;[25] sexuality is the first phenomenon of the inadequacy of self to self, the first effort to integrate the individual with the species larger than itself. The animal can be treated as a thing, but it is not a thing in the same sense as inert matter. It is a thing as the result of work

[23] Mikel Dufrenne, "Myth, Science et Ethique du sexe," *Esprit* (November 1960), p. 1708.
[24] P. Ricœur, "Merveille, Errance, Enigme," *Esprit* (November 1960), p. 1675.
[25] Bataille, *op. cit.*, and G. W. F. Hegel, *Précis de l'Encyclopédie des Sciences Philosophiques*, §§369, 370.

(cattle raising), or as a tool (draft animals). To treat the animal purely as a thing is to deny that it is animal, and it is animal precisely because of the sexual exuberance that draws it into the orbit of a species which endlessly reproduces itself. The inadequacy that marks individual reality becomes a tension, a desire which objectivizes the incommensurability of animal and thing.

"The species maintains itself only by the destruction of individuals who fulfill their destiny in the sexual act; if this destiny be no higher, they then go down to their death," wrote Hegel. But apart from this infinite procession, sexual anthropology intends to reveal the radical meaning of man and woman as beings. What is the significance of sexuality to these beings in whom freedom has taken the place of biological fate?

Sexual anthropology intends to recognize and reveal the deep significance of man and woman as beings. It seeks a meaning in order to discover an optimum line of development that would allow sexuality to exercise its highest humanizing virtues, if it has any, or to discover whether sexuality should be considered an obstacle to what is most human—an animal heritage, the voice of the species, if it is only animal and a hindrance to humanness. The difficulty is that animal origin and the voice of the blood are human dimensions, and that the discovery of this meaning is not in opposition to carnal freedom but in a tenuous unity with it.

What is it to be a man vis-à-vis a woman and a woman vis-à-vis a man, beyond the call to mate? The encounter of man and woman is not the encounter of male and female, or at least it is not this alone. Does the sexual relationship emanate from the personality or not? Or is it merely a reflection of the needs of the species on the personal level?

The questions asked on this level receive three types of answers, based on positions which are at times claimed to be self-evident, and are offered without proof.

SEXUALITY: INDIVIDUAL CHARACTER

A more or less conscious individualism in all that concerns sex is the accepted position of positive sociology. As Aristotle said of philosophy before his aphorism was applied to politics, not to philosophize is the worst philosophy. To limit oneself to the examination and classification of the social structures in which sexual relations take place, to compile statistics of admitted behavior, whether or not in conformity with institutions, is a useful and necessary undertaking. But a sociologist of Kinsey's type claims that he does not wish to answer our question, "What is it to be a man and what is it to be a woman? In fact he has already answered: he interrogates, acts, and investigates as though he already had evidence that mankind is composed of individuals who are sexed differently. He is already certain that there are two beings, two neighboring realities in keeping with two different points of view; he tends to consider each sex as rooted in a kind of "nature" (biological, psychological, social) proper to itself, and as though it were evident that each individual is complete in himself. Nothing is less certain! It is only a starting hypothesis that individuals would be sexed even without any encounter with the other sex, that each human individual is fundamentally a sexed being.

SEXUAL NEUTRALITY ON THE PERSONAL LEVEL

Contrary to the view just described, but this time in accordance with thinking based largely on existential phenomenology, each individual is fundamentally neuter if considered from the viewpoint of a sexuality that is truly human. "One is not born, one becomes, a woman," writes Simone de Beauvoir.[26] Men and women are beings created by society; society differentiates them. Following Husserl, many phenomenologists deny that there is any substantial characteristic of the human person; to them, the person is the activity by which one achieves self-fulfillment; one is what one becomes. Simone de Beauvoir, following Sartre, identifies the person with the existential project as it has come to be socially objectified. The person is entirely neutral, the value of the sexed body derives from social images. One becomes a man or becomes a

---

[26] Simone de Beauvoir, *The Second Sex*, H. M. Parshley, trans. and ed. (New York: Alfred A. Knopf, 1953; paperback, New York: Bantam Books, 1961), p. 249.

woman in the midst of the social relationships that characterize the struggle for existence and independence. The man-woman relationship is only one particular aspect of the master-slave dialectic. Woman's emancipation has brought up the problem in our day: an oppressed class has won admission to true humanity.

SEXUALITY AS A RELATIONSHIP AFFECTING PERSONS

It is legitimate to begin with a question in line with the prevailing trends of contemporary psychology: Instead of starting with individuals, whether neutral or sexed, should we not take the relationship itself as the fundamental object of analysis? Ought we to deal not with a separate person, but with a person in his relation to others? This would allow us to deal with a dimension essential to the person, the being-for-another, the man-woman relationship, the reciprocity of the sexes. It does not deal with the setting that creates the relationship, but with a fundamental relationship that creates varying personal situations.

The subject of sexual anthropology thus becomes the confrontation of man and woman; man is man only vis-à-vis man, woman is woman only vis-à-vis man. Despite the shift in roles and the transformation of values, we are not dealing with a social creation; human reality is defined by fundamental reciprocity, which itself is the datum to be analyzed.

We have no reason to take one position in preference to another. We will allow the object of our inquiry to guide us, trying only to discover what sexuality is, how it develops, and where its chances of success lie.

Our sole criterion is reason.[27]

27 This is not to say that we do not regard religious faith as important; this book ends with several pages on marriage as a sacrament. Nevertheless, it should be possible to aim at a rational approach to sexuality *per se*, our object being its human development.

CHAPTER TWO

The Relativity of the Sexes

Do biological data allow us to define sex as a characteristic of the individual?

Our first, unconsidered response would be affirmative. Before we make any judgment in the matter, a primitive feeling, rooted deep in our animal heritage, surely tells us of the presence of an individual of the opposite sex. This impulse, which seeps into our consciousness through all our nervous fibers, and social customs that allow us to objectify it, such as style and dress, has accustomed us to consider sex a perfectly definable individual characteristic—until we are asked to define it.

We now ask this question of the biologist: Is there an objective constant, a fixed biological characteristic which allows us with certainty and in all cases to define the sexual differences of a given individual on the biological level? His reply may appear disappointing: ordinarily, after referring to the relativity of the sexes, he stops short with the presence, the absence, or the difference of a single chromosome, thus underscoring the vagueness and uncertainty of the connection with what excites such deep emotions and attraction to the opposite sex.

The most evident morphological characteristics, those with the greatest capacity to excite eroticism, those that serve us daily to define a male or a female body, are not fundamental data. A simple treatment with hormones can cause women to grow beards; a tumor in the suprarenal glands can produce the same involuntary result. Atrophy of the mammary glands is produced just as easily, and the possibility of such alteration of so-called secondary characteristics is now well recognized.

But where does the genital function enter the definition? It is the traditional criterion, one particularly used by theologians and moralists since the Middle Ages; they had it from Aristotle and, they thought, common sense.

To answer our question, we must distinguish between genetic sex, genital sex, and hormonal sex, and examine how they are placed in relation to one another, until we either find or fail to find an objective constant by which to determine sex on the biological plane and for a given individual.[1]

GENETIC SEX

Genetic sex is, properly speaking, the sex of the primordial cell. This nuclear cell may have a male or a female structure.

Each of the gametes (reproductive cells) contains half of the chromosomes necessary to form a diploid nucleus; their union gives a single cell, an egg, which, by dividing into a number of cells, will by degrees form the complete organism. In most species the ovules are alike, whereas there are two kinds of spermatozoons, one which determines male sex, the other female sex. Among birds and butterflies, by contrast, the ovules are differentiated by a single chromosome; a chromosome with a haploid nucleus (having half the number of somatic cells) and usually coming from the spermatozoon, brings in the sexual variant.

In the human species, the nuclear cells normally contain 46 chromosomes, divided into 22 pairs of somatic chromosomes and two sex chromosomes. Each pair contains one chromosome from the mother and one from the father. The somatic chromosomes are multiplied by mitosis, or separation into two new identical parts, but the multiplication of the sexual cells (spermatogenesis in the male and oogenesis in the female) is effected by a process of reduction division, or meiosis. Each of the germ cells, male and female, has only half of the chromosome constitution of the adult; the diploid germ cells are transformed into haploid cells. Whereas each

[1] G. Bataille, "Qu'est-ce que le sexe?" *Critique* (April 1947), pp. 363–72 (quoted text on p. 366). This writer's reflections have guided us in writing this chapter; later advances in genetics have only confirmed his conclusions.

of the woman's cells is equipped with 22 pairs of somatic chromosomes plus two chromosomes we shall call X (XX), the haploid cells contain only a simple series of 22 chromosomes plus one chromosome X. Since the chromosome constitution of the man is one chromosome X and one chromosome Y (XY), the masculine haploid cell can contain either 22 chromosomes plus X or 22 chromosomes plus Y.

All cell divisions can present anomalies. It can happen that, instead of separating, two elements enter together into one daughter cell, whereas none may enter another. At the end of meiosis (crossing over) some ovules may carry two X, others none; some spermatozoids may carry two chromosomes XY, others none. Fertilization may produce individuals whose chromosome equipment is a single X, others XXY, others XXX. Despite anomalies which have received rather careful study, it can be said that the presence of the Y chromosome normally determines male sex. This is to say that the chromosome Y induces genital male development, whereas in its absence it seems that development goes spontaneously in the female direction. Such is genetic sex, which is of such decisive importance.[2]

GENITAL SEX

Genital (or gonadic) sex is determined by its generative function. It is defined by its role in the reproduction of the species, a role itself conditioned by the sex apparatus properly so called, or gonad (primary sex gland), according to whether this organ produces male or female gametes, namely spermatozoids or ovules.

In the human embryo, sex remains undifferentiated until the ninth week. Certain cells group themselves in the latero-vertebral region, which has a peripheral (cortical) zone capable of forming ovaries and a central (medullary) part capable of forming testes.

In principle, genital sex corresponds to genetic sex. The latter, it seems, is predominant and if, from natural causes or through intervention, genital sex is reversed in relation to genetic sex, the

[2] J. Lafourcade, "La Détermination du sexe dans l'espèce humaine et ses anomalies," *Cahiers Laënnec* (June 1962), pp. 3-36.

latter is ready to lead the genital back to the original sex. However, stable reversals have been obtained.

HORMONAL SEX

The genital glands, or more exactly the cells in the tissue surrounding the testicular tubes or the follicles of the ovary, secrete all male or female hormones, but in different proportions. The cortico-suprarenal gland also produces hormones similar in chemistry to sex hormones. A certain harmony in the proportion of these hormones is what produces secondary characteristics, such as the breaking of the male voice at puberty or the development of mammary glands in the female.

The chemistry of male and female hormones is similar; there are also intermediate hormones which are chemically the same in all vertebrates. They come from the body, or *soma*, and not from the germ cells.

Genetic sex appears to have the role of a factorial element operating by means of hormone secretions. Hormonal sex in fact conditions not only the development but the activation of genetic sexuality, and the erotic capacities of every organism, particularly the nervous system, also derive from it.[3]

RELATIVITY OF THE SEXES

What is the invariable way to define sex? Hormonal sex is the source and condition of eroticism, but it is fragile and plastic. Gonadic sex is also modifiable. It is easy to develop the ovaries of a young chicken by injecting female hormones. In the batrachians (toads and frogs), a complete reversal of sex can be easily produced. No doubt the results of such experimentation are far from satisfactory for those who would like to determine the genital sex of a child; total reversal is seldom achieved, and in the human species the risk of producing a monster is too great. However, genital sex is

[3] On this triple definition of sexuality, cf. P. Chauchard, *La Vie sexuelle*, "Que sais-je?" series (Paris: P.U.F., 1965), pp. 15 ff.

itself all too malleable to be accepted as a fundamental characteristic of the individual.

The biologist tends to define fundamental sexuality by genetic
sex. Genital sex can, of course, be the reverse of genetic sex, but
why prefer the first to the second? After the transformation of a
genetically male frog into a genitally female frog, Etienne Wolff
spoke of crossing two males.[4] We still speak of true or false males,
true or false females, but what is the meaning of true or false? Why
is genetic sex the criterion?

> Moreover, [writes George Bataille] genetic sex no longer has the
> last word. Etienne Wolff cites the case of a twenty-five-year-old
> individual who outwardly presented characteristics of both sexes
> (male in general formation of the body and sexual organs, but
> with a bursa containing only one testis; with female breasts, smooth
> skin and hairless face). This individual had suffered for several
> years periodic pains which justified an abdominal operation. At
> that time female sex elements were discovered, including a func-
> tioning ovary. Following the removal of the ovary, there was a
> rapid change in the individual; at the end of a few days the breasts
> flattened out, the face was covered with down and the voice became
> deeper. Etienne Wolff nevertheless admitted that this individual
> was in all probability of female genetic sex.[5]

Since 1953 it has been easy to diagnose genetic sex, and we are
no longer uncertain on this score. We are now able to discover
anomalies in the combination of sexual chromosomes, so that we
may no longer speak of the probable predominance of one sex over
the other. In the above case, moreover, we must note that the
scientist himself chose genital sex as his criterion! Many anomalies
of this order, with ambiguity of secondary sexual characteristics,
have been verified.

Sexuality seems to be a stabilizing factor related directly to hormonal balance. The only fundamental characteristic of the individual is genetic sex. Yet this same genetic sex seems nothing more

[4] E. Wolff, *Les Changements de sexe* (Paris: Gallimard, 1946).
[5] G. Bataille, in *Critique*, April 1947.

than the fundamental factor of a dubious hormonal evolution. Etienne Wolff agreed when he wrote: "The genetic constitution has only a weak and variable effect in differentiating sex." Genital and genetic sex are, of course, generally in continuity on the animal level, although this stability is not conclusive and was acquired only slowly in the course of evolution. This stability was late to appear and remains too tenuous for us to say that genetic sex is fundamental in defining the sex of the individual.

In the lower species, genital sex is highly variable; there are many examples. The *bonnelia viridis*, a marine worm found on the coasts of the Mediterranean, is male or female according to whether or not it attaches itself to the proboscis of the mother: secretions from the proboscis have a masculinizing effect. *Crepidula*, a mollusk found on the coasts of America, lives piled up on empty shells. At the bottom of the pile live the oldest, always female; in the middle are the intersexed; the youngest are on top and are always male. An annelid such as *ophryotroca puerilis* is male or female according to the number of its segments. The youngest is always male and remains so if, by dissection it is kept to less than 15 segments; if it acquires 15 to 20 segments, it becomes female. But if two adult females are isolated, the youngest, the least feminized, again transforms itself into a male. It is startling to see these sexual cells transform themselves, according to the case, into ovocytes or spermatocytes.[6]

The functions alone are differentiated; one cannot discuss the production, instantaneous or not, of male gametes and female gametes. Must we then say with another biologist: "This production of male or female gametes is the essential factor, the primary characteristic of sexuality. It is necessarily completed by attraction to the other sex, by the libido which will make relations possible and probable"[7]?

It is always hazardous to attribute a function of this kind to an individual. To say of an individual animal that it produces ovules and is therefore female is to designate a quality which is unstable, but which in the higher species (vertebrates) is stabilized as growth

[6] J. Carles, *La Sexualité* (Paris: A. Colin, 1953), pp. 27–8.
[7] *Ibid.*, p. 17.

proceeds, although it can never be defined in terms of ultimately fixed characteristics.

Sex as the attribute of an individual remains beyond definition. On this level the absence, the difference, even the reduplication of one chromosome remains all that is definitive, without being an absolutely determining factor.

George Bataille draws two conclusions from these analyses:

"Sex," he writes, "is only a characteristic analogous to the solid or liquid condition of the body." This conclusion does not seem to me well founded; it is really valid only in reference to hormonal sex. If we stress genital sex, the conclusion would seem to be necessary that there is a reciprocity of functions, a variable reciprocity affecting and modifying the individual. In no case is sex an "essence"; we have to remember this when people speak to us of male or female "nature."

Bataille's second conclusion seems fundamental: "Science breaks down into interactions what primary human experience had viewed as substances. The only view of things that science will support is a continuous communication in which beings and things are lost (thus love, if we give this name to the conjuction of beings, is considered a primary datum, but not man or woman)."[8] Without hazarding one more extrapolation to man and woman, let us say that in the evolution of living beings sexuality appears as a variable relationship and is defined as a relationship. Although the species is the direct object of this relationship, the individual is deeply affected by it. Does sexuality have no individual basis in the animal world? Does it have such a basis in man? It would seem that any such basis must be sought elsewhere than in man's animal roots and background.

We have long heard talk of "gradations" and of the "relativity" of sex, ideas difficult to fit into our ways of speech. They upset a number of static images based on unreasoned sentiments, on custom, and on the male fear of losing one of the foundations of his superiority by surrendering the absolute character of the organ that makes him "male." But, biologically speaking, we cannot speak of maleness or femaleness as characteristics that are fixed and de-

[8] G. Bataille, in *Critique*, April 1947.

fined in isolated individuals; we are dealing rather with the reciprocity of functions. Sexuality is a relation that characterizes the variable condition of the animal world so that each individual is sexually defined by this very relationship. But to biologists, sex is not a datum that characterizes the individual; they treat it rather as a relationship in the species.

CHAPTER THREE

Animal Sexuality and Human Sexuality

Animal sexuality and human sexuality aim at the reproduction of the species and can be so compared, but human sexuality largely transcends this purpose. The modes of reproduction of plants and animals show vast variations. Sexuality is just one particular method of reproduction, its complex role having been late to appear in the succession of the species. It manifested itself only when a certain level of organization had been reached. It marked the beginning of an inverse mechanism of reproduction. There had been cell division, and schizogenesis or fission. Reproduction had been effected by the division of one individual into two new and similar ones. Sexuality, on the other hand, leads to the conjugation of two individualized gametes, two haploid cells, into a single new cell; it permits a far broader range of mutations and makes a great variety in natural selection possible, by accumulating in the genes a large variety of information which can be passed on to the new cell.[1]

ANIMAL SEXUALITY

Animal sexuality develops in a manner that is literally senseless. Despite assertions to the contrary of certain enthusiastic observers,

[1] Cf. Lamotte, "La Théorie actuelle des mécanismes de l'Évolution," *Archives de Philosophie*, Vol. XIII, cahier 1 (January 1–March 1960), p. 19: "The continuous combination of genes determined by sexuality in populating the species increases considerably . . . the source of variations which mutations already constitute of themselves. It is from such combinations that mutations derive a large part of their evolutionary force, because this addition to genetic variability is put to work in populations with a rapidity and efficiency infinitely superior to that of isolated mutations. The genetic 'plasticity' which it gives to the species reaches almost unimaginable proportions."

no sense or direction is shown other than a dynamism that explodes in all directions. There is unlimited waste in the tremendous spread and dissemination of germs, from which only two among thousands succeed in fusing to create a new plant or a new animal. In this complex growth of sexual varieties a whole series of interactions take place which on the surface appear fantastic and meaningless: the bee mingling with the flowers, sexual parades and dances of birds, or monstrous and fantastic copulations in which the male is often the victim. The female of certain insects must destroy the abdomen of the male in order to ingest the spermatozoids. The species is the winner, transmission of life is what counts; the male is often narrowly restricted to his function: he fertilizes, and dies.

We sometimes hear discussion of the autoregulation of animal instinct, which in man is replaced by voluntary control. Such statements exaggerate the importance of very limited observations: this alleged autoregulation is no more than a restriction of copulation to the rutting period and an adjustment, sometimes highly complex, of the copulatory organs of the male to those of the female. The evolution of sexuality poses exactly the same problems as the evolution of the species in which it came to play a fundamental role. But all integration supposes in the interplay of large numbers a certain number of perfect coincidences. An equilibrium arises which is equivalent to regulation, but on the level of the species. When voluntary control replaces this specific equilibrium, no continuity is evident; and even if comparison remains possible it is not meaningful. No such regulation or pattern is evident among existing anthropoids. In 1942, Carpenter's observations of 409 rhesus monkeys, set free on the island of Santiago off Puerto Rico, gave evidence of variations in sexual behavior. Many confirmations of these observations followed, showing moreover that among the group left at liberty, with opportunity for stimuli and immediate copulation, there were cases of what we call masturbation, homosexuality, incest, etc.

HUMAN SEXUALITY

Viewed simply as one branch of the primates, man is a species of animal, and the human being continues to display the same sexuality as other mammals. But as human sexuality, it also shows a break with animal nature. Here as elsewhere, the discussion is sometimes vitiated by recourse to that ambiguous word *nature*, which by its range of meanings can just as easily refer to animal organism as to rationality. We do not always know what the moralist is thinking of when he refers to what is "natural" in human sexuality. If we assert that animal nature and human nature are not continuous, the word protean still requires definition. If human nature means autonomy to act freely—the subject's rationality—animal nature suggests, on the contrary, the image of conditioning. The transition from animal to human nature can only be negation, the transcendence of determinisms and opposition to them. Man is endowed with autonomy and can choose to adopt a position over and against nature, that is, the material world, as well as over and against his own animal nature.[2] Such is the man-nature struggle, whether nature be inorganic or organic; and the human reality may be self drawn up against self, but is never so entirely; rather, it is the act of assuming this position.

There is conflict as well as continuity.

We are an animal species; the vital urge of an instinct that has become conscious persists and grows in us. It is the powerful magnetism of our roots, rising both from the strength and the source of the species; it is both abyss and foundation. This instinct is a latent desire, not always admitted but always there, sometimes shamefully repressed but springing up again in various guises to take part in the orgiastic delirium of nature. There is, indeed, a human aspect of animal sexuality in the orgiastic feast, the bacchanal.

This is not to say that the bacchanal was wholly sexual in

[2] This is not the place to raise controversies about "human nature." It is nevertheless opportune to emphasize that the words do not mean simply membership in the cosmos through the intermediary of the living world. "Traditionally, but in less emphatic fashion than today, to consider man as *one* nature and not as an essence, is to consider man not as an immovable idea but in the concrete exercise of his act of being. Thus man emerges with freedom to assume the risks of the future. Man is a thinking being. What does this mean other than that he recognizes the determinisms of the past as historical free exercise? Man is a historical being, in this sense he has a human nature. To affirm or deny the existence of human nature is to affirm or deny the meaning of his history." A. Jeannière, "L'homme peut-il modifier l'homme?" *Revue de l'Action Populaire*, No. 162 (November 1962), p. 1061.

significance, but inversely, the first properly human meaning given to sexuality appeared in the phallic cults where it was associated with the cosmic forces that lead the frenzied dance of the life-and-death cycles. Sexuality drew its meaning from that cosmic dimension by which man participated in a vital energy that transcended him, expending himself in the dissemination of life and returning in death to the indefinite cycles of nature.

To take a Greek example, the first Ionic philosophers gave as the principle of *physis* the following: the wind that is also the breath and the soul; water—the well in the oasis, the fickle sea, the spongy fermentation of life in the swamps; fire—the lightning flash and the piercing eye; all of them elements whose turbulence and intensity would explain the frenzied dynamism of both plant and animal life and the law to which their cycles are subject. But well before the human mind first attempted to put these ideas into a rational order, sexuality had a share in those forces from which it seemed to emanate.

Sex, then, was first revealed as sacred because the fundamental forces of nature were held sacred. It was a mode of participation in nature, communion between man and nature; it was not yet in any sense communion between man and woman. In the beginning it took several forms; but apart from games and daily routines—often without norms or any special significance for the tribe beyond the complex laws regulating the exchange of women and the family structure—the sexual act was above all a ritual act, performed by the young couple in the furrow before the sowing, or liturgically celebrated in the temple with a religious prostitute.[3]

"The festival of spring broke the human order of *praxis* to *repeat* with nature the first gestures denoting elementary need (food, love), to *resurrect* the divine and cosmic lost in the City by the Logos—to *identify itself* with cosmic rhythms in an act, a serious game."[4] These cycles, and cycles of divinely regulated cycles, represented the renewal of the sun, the moon, the seasons; man took

[3] Mikel Dufrenne, "Mythe, Science et Ethique du Sexe," *Esprit* (November 1960), p. 1703.

[4] Henri Lefebvre, *Introduction à la modernité* (Paris: Éditions de Minuit, 1963), p. 149.

part in the cosmic drama, animating it by the sacral action of the orgy, but it could also happen that salvation appeared at the end to release him from the infernal round.

The same nostalgia and the same need for unity survived throughout the course of history and the refinement of social life. The spring festivals reappeared in the Middle Ages, disciplined and socialized into the Feasts of May—and the Virgin took the place of Aphrodite.

In daily life there was no real encounter between man and woman. Marriage was established according to the laws of exchange; its regulations were purely social and of an economic nature, for the exchange of women between tribes, or within the tribe, which remained the center of economic reference. Claude Lévi-Strauss has shown that the prohibition of incest, a fundamental law for such exchange and for gifts between clans, was a necessary condition for the transition from nature to culture, or, if one prefers, from the animal to the human realm. The humanization of the man-woman relationship presupposes the transcendence of sexuality in social structures before love became possible or even imaginable.[5]

Human love does not appear as a sublimation of sexuality, the encounter of the animal pair as accomplished in the human couple. There is no encounter in animal mating; in the animal world the individual exists only for the species. When two human

[5] We cannot admit, as is sometimes suggested, that exogamy might have been the result of the observation of the often defective character of consanguineous unions. As a matter of fact, a large number of societies advocated marriages between collateral cousins which would involve the same dangers as marriages forbidden between lineal cousins.

"The prohibition of incest was less a law forbidding a man to marry his mother, sister, or daughter than a law which obliged him to give his mother, sister, or daughter to another. It was the all-important law for making gifts" (Claude Lévi-Strauss, *Les structures élémentaires de la parenté* [Paris: P.U.F., 1949], p. 596). But a gift called for a gift in return. At the very basis of the man-woman relationship we find already a system of exchange. These relations between the sexes were "the methods of a great function of communication which also included language" (p. 613). The reasons for the prohibition of incest and exogamy were "the establishment of a bond between men without which they could not have raised themselves above biological organization in order to achieve social organization" (p. 612).

persons come together, they invent a union which can be expressed and confirmed by sexuality, but sexuality neither suggested nor prepared them for this union. Animal sexuality does not achieve meaning in human sexuality; on the contrary, man gives meaning to animal sexuality.

> It does not seem that love arose as a sublimation of sexuality, it was invented by mankind little by little; at a time when it scarcely held a place in ancient mythologies as a passion which dedicated one being to another and burned or devoured him, spiritual intensity was substituted for the vital frenzy. Such love was not a metamorphosis of sexuality nor an avatar of the libido: Orpheus and Tristan had no infancy. But they encountered sexuality and immediately submitted to it; they sought a means of expression: to possess the body was to assure possession of the soul. Thereafter sexuality became meaningful to the extent that it appeared as an aspect of love, and consecrated by it.[6]

Human love is not an invention based on sexuality. It is the result of a slow flowering, it needed gradual education by the prohibition of incest, which had its motives not in the sexual order but came from social life and its economy; it needed the slow maturation of culture and history. Human love makes sexuality its servant, it is not a sublimation of sexuality. If there is a sublimation of animal sexuality, it can be found only along the lines manifested by eroticism.

EROTICISM

There is one human manifestation of animal sexuality, and that is eroticism.

Many writers emphasize the aspect of eroticism that marks it as a retrogression to the infantile stages of sexual life. "Eroticism varies with place and time. In present-day Western civilization it plays a large part in literature, art, cinema, etc. It consists in a collective concern with a form of vital sexuality that is most often degraded by the immaturity or infantilism of sexual desire."[7]

There is, however, a lucid and deliberate eroticism, defined by

[6] Dufrenne, *op. cit.*, p. 1704.
[7] A. Hesnard, *Esprit* (November 1960), p. 1821.

Georges Bataille as "approbation of life even in death."[8] This approbation is freely bestowed; it makes everything subservient to life as it explodes in sexuality, including the human partner and sometimes even one's own ego.

In considering eroticism, one becomes all the more aware that love exists in discontinuity with animal sexuality and not continuous with it; human continuity of animal sexuality does indeed exist in eroticism, but eroticism is the negation of love.

Eroticism is the search for sensual pleasure in the immediate satisfaction of desire—but in a human manner. It is not a simple abandonment to animal drives, but accepts sensual pleasure as its law and mental purpose. Consequently, it will appear in the human subject with the ambiguity of a dual aspect: it both denies and spiritualizes.

It spiritualizes. It truly humanizes animal sexuality. In proportion as a sensuality that wills to be human wills at the same time to be total, it must necessarily acquire the power to destroy. Eroticism is the development of a need, and as such desires the object to which it is drawn, and wills to possess it. It cannot be a pure and solitary transcendence of self. But it transcends every object in this sensual pleasure which wills to be total; and the transcendence takes effect in the destruction of the object. Such transcendence wills to be human; its favorite object is woman, who must necessarily be destroyed as woman (as which she is necessary), then destroyed as object; that is, unless we are lost with her in the enchantment of a desire deep enough to come from the depths of our nature and our biological past, and violent enough to lead us to the loss of self. Yet the intermediate and social stages of this process involve precisely the humanization of the object. One of the results, for example, will be the erotization of the entire human body and even of dress. It is hard to grasp this development, but it is a rather recent phenomenon and not yet as universal as erotization of the human face.

Eroticism is carried beyond itself by the very movement and gestures it engenders. Edgar Morin has written thus about the kiss:

[8] *L'Érotisme* (Paris: Éditions de Minuit, 1957), p. 17.

Motion picture stars have exalted the kiss on the mouth where it was known, or have introduced it where it was not. The kiss is not only the key-technique of love-making, or the cinematographic substitute for the sexual embrace which is forbidden by censorship; it is the twentieth century's reigning symbol of the role of face and soul in love. The kiss goes with eroticism of the face, and both were unknown in antiquity and are still ignored by certain civilizations. The kiss is not merely the discovery of a new tactile sensual pleasure. It revives forgotten myths that identify the soul with breath and symbolizes communion or symbiosis of soul. The kiss, then, is not only the salt and spice added to all Western films; it is the profound expression of a love that eroticizes the soul and mysticizes the body.[9]

The aspiration of Eros is to identify its final purpose with the ultimate repose that restores original peace after all conflicts are past. And of course the end is immediate; it is there, captured in the very instant. But the impulse has repercussions in a series of captivating and fugitive moments; it reaches beyond those moments to the end of the individual's incompleteness. Erotic dynamism aims to equate the object of love with the Whole, and in the end leads to a kind of divinization of the "female object," personalized by identification with Nature herself. Woman finds herself bound to the cosmos by agrarian cultures which included these bonds in stereotypes that authenticated the parallel between sexuality and the living world; woman becomes the Whole and truly woman as she symbolizes nature. Erotic ecstasy seeks a humanized form of primitive unity, the reconciliation of man with nature and with himself. "You can make love with the whole universe, alone, alone with one woman," wrote Pierre Emmanuel. "Woman is put before him [the man] as the attraction and the symbol of the world. And because the world is always larger and always unfinished and always in advance of us, man, in order to grasp his love, finds himself engaged in a never-ending conquest of the universe and of himself. In this sense, man will never attain to woman save in the consummation of the universal Union."[10] The

9 Edgar Morin, *Les Stars* (Paris: Éditions du seuil, 1957), p. 179.
10 Pierre Teilhard de Chardin, "Construire la Terre," in *Cahiers Pierre Teilhard de Chardin*, No. 1 (Paris: Éditions du Seuil, 1958), pp. 14-15.

quoted passage shows the normal transposition of sublimations: the origin is placed at the end, the beginning of the cleavage is put after the conflicts. Return to the primordial state is perceived more and more clearly as a passage to a state in which conflicts have been resolved, as a genuine union and no longer as the primitive fusion. In contrast to Teilhard's view, eroticism often dispenses with the mediation of history and dreams of an immediate fusion that drags freedom down into the same abyss from which it springs.

Was not this the deeper meaning of religious prositution, to restore the primeval harmony of "once upon a time"—mythological time, the time that founded time before all human history—when man was united with nature and with himself? Was it not to actualize the presence of the holy that marks the age of myth?

But eroticism does not always proceed, nor proceed directly, to the confrontation with love; it denies at the same time as it spiritualizes. In its desire for totality, eroticism, which accepts sensual pleasure as its law, does not draw the individual out of his own ego, but leads to negation of the partner. Whereas animal sexuality produces a brief conjunction of beings on the simple biological level where they are entirely situated, the man who seeks the same immediate unity with nature obtains the contrary of what he desires; he will separate himself from his partner precisely because she is a subject who cannot and will not be ruled as an object by the will of another. As he cuts himself off from his partner, he cuts himself off from nature. Even Georges Bataille, in his keen analysis of eroticism, wants to consider woman the object. But no matter what he says and in spite of all distinctions, woman is herself, she is a subject, and that is why eroticism leads to conflict or failure or both. When communion with universal nature is sought in a particular woman, it escapes along with her. Such is the ambiguous unfolding of animal sexuality and its sublimation today, outside of the religious sphere where it made its first appearance.

The writings of De Sade bear witness to the destructive effects of an eroticism carried to the extremes of conscious paroxysm. De Sade merely enlarged reactions that commonly go no further

than fantasy and are usually not admitted; eroticism here be-
trays that it tends toward death and not toward communion—
even if not with another being, at least with oneself in some
nonexistent nature. Centered on an ego that seeks concrete and
immediate universalization, eroticism falls back into the abyss
from which it springs; it returns to nothingness. "My only rule
of conduct is that I choose everything that makes me happy and
I don't care a rap if what I choose is bad for others."[11] Here
the center of desire asserts itself in all its isolation. The human
sublimation of animal sexuality leads to an end which is the
opposite of love; not to union—even to the passing union of two
beings—but to isolation.

Eroticism certainly fails to achieve its end (does love?), at any
rate, its movement is contrary to that of love. Thus, as Georges
Bataille stressed, "the true nature of sexual attraction can be revealed only in literature which portrays impossible characters
and scenes. Otherwise it would remain concealed, since the pure
sexual act could not be recognized in the fog of tenderness, because
ordinarily love means communication, and by its very name is
linked to the existence of another person."[12] This is the reason,
as Bataille says further, why "to praise De Sade is to sentimentalize
his thought."

Eroticism may believe that it leads to affirmation of self by
negation of the other; this was De Sade's illusion. Without illusion, as in Georges Bataille, it seeks at one and the same time
the loss of self and of the other; it is a drive toward death, toward
the ecstatic taste of nothingness. Georges Bataille compares it to
mystical experience—a valid comparison, it seems to me, only to
the extent that the two experiences are diametrically opposed.
Nothingness, which is always sought in the heart of man, the
only place of its revelation, can just as well be a call to the world's
depths as to what lies beyond the world. It remains true that
mystical experience can be expressed only in erotic language;
whether or not it leads to increased humanness is another ques-

[11] Maurice Blanchot, quoted by Georges Bataille in "Le bonheur, érotisme
et la littérature," *Critique* (May 1949), p. 404.
[12] *Ibid.*, p. 405.

tion which must be left open. The accounts we have been given of voyages to the end of the self and the darkness sometimes leave us with the agonizing question: "Is this end also the empty tomb?" The paths, at any rate, head in opposite directions, and what is of interest to us here in the world of men, the unfolding of animal sexuality is clearly the destruction of love.

SEXUALITY AND PRACTICE

There is conflict also between sexual activity and work. Work is an indirect way of entering into relation with nature, sexuality is an immediate way. Man lives in an organized society and sexuality is the very negation of this organization. To accept sensual pleasure and the search for sexual enjoyment as rules for action appears to be in conflict with the rational organization of civic life. Sexual pleasure, emanating from deep animality, is both fascinating and frightening to the extent that it seems to promise unity with nature as such, rather than an indirect and difficult unity with nature transformed by work. The primal unity is that of the lost Paradise, the unity that existed before man appeared; the cleavage by which the spirit is divided and turned against itself is obliterated in the intoxication that makes one forget the torpor which accompanies or follows that cleavage.

But sexuality imbues all human behavior; indirect or otherwise, unity is always a promise that cannot be fulfilled. Sex is repressed by social life, but it also happens that we denounce the rules of social life, "the conventions of the day," as Georges Bataille calls them, or "the law of the day" as Hegel says, to proclaim "the truth of the night" (Bataille) or "the law of the night" (Hegel). A dialogue could be held between authentically human sexuality and the social order. As an expression of love, sexuality can reveal the depths of certain human bonds that are neglected in civic life. It was in this sense that Hegel reinterpreted the myth of Antigone and its appeal to the unwritten laws of the home against decrees of the state. But sexuality can also be a simple assertion of nature in its immediacy, an aspiration toward nothingness which assumes the stance of the Whole it denies;

then it does nothing save open up the road to failure. "In fact, if things are viewed in their elementary aspect, nothing is perceived at first except a clear delimitation. Sexual behavior and communal behavior are mutually exclusive. There are two incompatible worlds, the world of erotic acts, the other of the various actions of societal life. No doubt paths lead from the first to the second, but they are never smooth."[13]

Insofar as sexuality is eroticism and approbation "of life unto death," it can be contrasted with humanizing work and the primacy given to work. We may also contrast a sexuality subordinated to human love with work that alienates and dehumanizes, and give primacy to love—for love, like work, can lead to alienation. But is there a conflict between human sexuality and humanizing work? In both cases, relations are established and unions formed in the midst of conflict and opposition. Between the two ways of relating to nature there is no longer any alternative except dialogue and history. Love and work cannot be understood outside their historical linkage, they are their own history. This is why, when we abstract the sexual dimension of man in order to analyze amorous and sexual behavior and its social repercussions in greatly different cultures, we get the impression that we are not analyzing the same reality, or else are faced with a variety of manifestations of human sexuality which greatly exceeds the diversity found in the animal world.

SEXUALITY AND FREEDOM

Human sexuality seems in conflict with animal sexuality, and at the same time capable of being lost in it. Only as a sexual being does man most universally experience the fact of belonging to an animal species. "The free self posits itself in opposition to the natural self: the most obscure point of the natural self is sex, and man feels that he must confront nature if he wishes to confront his own 'nature' and the 'need of the species'; man feels that since he is free to master himself he should also be free to master sexu-

13 Bataille, *op. cit.*, p. 402.

ality."[14] Arising from beyond myself—from that point where my nature is both abyss and foundation, the depths of the species— sexuality admits me only for the sake of the species, and only as an individual. This is the exact point where I can affirm the strength of my own autonomous and personal position, or where I can renounce and lose myself in a nature that is mine but outside myself, and transcends me only in order to crush me.

But opposition can also be grounded on more highly evolved levels than primordial instinct. We find in history more than one revealing phenomenon of this opposition. There are typical and significant instances which mark a new appraisal and at the same time constitute a stage in our present-day modes of the love encounter. Courtly love, already referred to elsewhere, again serves as an example. At the same time that love invented itself, it freed itself from the flesh.[15] Love was born at the dawn of European civilization within a master-slave dialectic; before its discoveries spread through all classes of society, it required a distinction in class between the lover and his inaccessible lady. Such was the true inaccessibility of the beloved that the gift of her body appeared not high above, not as the end of tenderness and the gift of hearts, not as the consecration of acts that preceded the decisive confrontation, but beneath, and more as an obstacle to be surmounted than as something to be achieved. The sword or the child who separated the lovers when finally night found them together in the same bed was less a guarantee than a symbol. Here the gift of the body came to seem a lack of love, evidence of a lapse into lasciviousness. The point was not only to increase the distance between the sexual need and its satsifaction—which was already to humanize it—but to mark the difference in origin between love and procreation. In one of its aspects courtly love went beyond the sexual difference between man and woman to establish there the fraternal friendship which had originally appeared among men. At another stage of history we find the prohibition of incest which suggested Claude Lévi-Strauss' reflections

[14] Michel Deguy, in reply to questionnaire of *Esprit* (November 1960), pp. 1691–92. We note that nature is here used simply to designate the needs of the species.

[15] René Nelli, *L'Érotique des troubadours* (Toulouse: Privat, 1963), p. 177.

on the subject. True love between man and woman, the reciprocal exchange of the gift of the body, presupposes the transcendence of desire. The integration of Eros into human love assumes that this transcendence has already occurred in another man-woman relation, the brother-sister relation.[16]

But when integration is total, love finds its language in eroticism, sexuality unfolds as it finds meaning, making itself the expression of a union that it can suggest but cannot bring to life. Neither a characteristic of the sexed individual, nor simply a biological function, nor pure physical determinism, sexuality becomes a dimension of human liberty even while it is the abyss from which liberty arose and into which it can sink down again and be lost. It cannot be identified with the generative need which it transcends when the species is no longer the end of the human person, nor with the libido insofar as it is the expression as well as the sublimation of the highest personal sphere. If sensual pleasure is the primary law of sexuality, it drags man down to orgiastic ecstasy and death; if ruled by the spirit, it is a dimension of all human communion.

As a dimension of human freedom, and of human communion, sexuality cannot be cut off from its history. Its occasional repercussions show themselves in the genesis of society, where it appears ever more clearly as a new way of relating to nature, and as the privileged expression of freedom in its attempt to unite with the other.

[16] Gaston Fessard, "Le Mystère de la société," *Recherches de Science religieuse* (2d trimester, 1948), pp. 194–95.

CHAPTER FOUR

Masculine and Feminine: Biological Symbols, Psychoanalytical Differentiation

From sexuality we turn back to love, to the search for partners who remain partners, and to the real otherness which exists at the heart of unity. Each of us would like to see the other as a person who is truly present, and as the person for him. Man and woman as sexual partners are in active relation with one another and with the world. The major obstacle we have to face is a long catalogue of ideas which, although approved by theologians and educators, are as obsolete as the Ptolemaic system.

BIOLOGICAL SYMBOLS

Sexual difference is based on the body and physiological characteristics, even of this difference cannot be said to determine an individual's destiny or to orient his freedom. Here it is a matter not only of the sexual organ but of sexual activity. Human beings define their sex, in fact, through their sexual activity as either masculine or feminine in their relation one to the other, and give meaning to that relation.

Such an idea is, of course, correct and fairly simple. But our commentary must not isolate the terms of this sexual relation, and not end up by defining a difference in natures, claiming that man has such and such a role in the sexual relation, and woman another role. . . . It is by no means sufficient to determine conditions of existence in order to define a finality which, moreover, is such that it often leads logically to defining two animal species of the same genus: namely, human beings.

The activity of man and the passivity of woman are often merely psychological transpositions of the symbolic meaning given to phallus and vagina. The transposition can be more or less direct, more or less determinative. Allusions to primary symbols of penetration and receptivity, possession and welcome, even conquest and captivity, often do no more than support traditional conceptions of the roles proper to man and woman. The gestures of mating are transposed to all aspects of behavior in human life, together with the possible (and often pernicious) influence of such images on the technique of love itself. Taking more account of the complexity of their own history, the symbols of psychoanalysis make further distinctions, but they, too, risk implanting notions that are static and stereotyped, as we shall see further on.

But, attempts have also been made to trace these symbols to a more remote origin. The destiny of the male is already determined, and in some ways signified, by the flagellate morphology of the spermatozoon. A kind of explosive protoplasm, the spermatozoon makes its way vigorously toward the ovule, which is stationary, and pierces the protecting membrane. According to this image, man will be more egocentric; what counts for him is action and the exercise of his mental or muscular powers.

The woman will be altercentric. Her sexuality is more diffused, less localized. The ovule's form is spheroid, which means that its direction and objective is not prescribed by morphology. Hence woman is a static being, and her action is manifested as a form of influence, a radiation, an inner energy acting by surface polarization.

Man will find fulfillment in trying to change the world. For him the world is the main object of knowledge and action. The woman will find fulfillment in *being*; she has more influence as the result of what she is than of what she does.

To all this why not add the openness of man's nature and the secretiveness of woman's? Also the logical temperament of the male (a form of possessive knowledge for the mastery of nature) and feminine intuition (an inner radiation, connaturalness with nature, a congenital compatibility which draws her more spontaneously toward beings and things).

In its imaginary and symbolic form, this line of thought is drearily materialistic, but its exponents believe that it escapes the stigma of materialism by the imagined sublimation or acceptance of an episodic act as determinative of life and character. Why should organs, or even gametes, define a temperament, a psychology of "natures"? Let us stop defining the spirit according to sexual cells; better still to believe that the spermatozoon alone contained the germ and that the ovule was merely its nourishment; then it was written, and obviously by God, that woman was made for man. The theologians of course added, "and man was made for God." Actually, as we have seen, even in the biological sphere we are always dealing with interactions. But to pass from biological interaction to a personal interrelation is a shift which is not only dangerous but necessarily false and purely imaginary in its materialistic simplicity. The biological conditions of existence in no wise define a free appraisal of relationship to the world and to one's ego.

PSYCHOANALYTICAL DIFFERENTIATION

The psychoanalyst defines sexuality by its genesis, and starts with early childhood. For the little girl the oral stage is prolonged by fixation on the mother; next she identifies herself with father. The feminine transposition of the Oedipus complex is the Electra complex, less sharply defined in structure than the Oedipus because the little girl's first fixation was on the mother, whereas the boy was not sexually attracted to the father. The boy will change the structure of his complex, but the mother will remain the objective of his libido. The girl's orientation will change and she will turn from the mother to fixation first on the father, then on the man. Thus in her a homosexual phase precedes the heterosexual phase. The drama occurs when she discovers the anatomical difference between the sexes, a discovery that produces a castration complex. Wishing to identify herself with her father, the little girl suffers by feeling herself different, and at the same time she feels rivalry with her mother. The most important event of her puberty is menstruation, a traumatic experience. She feels anger, inferiority, and shame: the Electra complex has again come to the surface. But this time the woman is in a position to accept or refuse her condition.

Helene Deutsch[1] following Freud, brings out three characteristic tendencies of women: narcissism, passivity, and masochism.

Narcissism is an echo of childhood homosexuality. Whereas the boy's sexuality is more active and seeks exterior achievement, the girl is absorbed in reveries centered on and around her ego, principally because her sexuality is more diffused and does not necessarily link her dreams of ideal love to genital activity. Despite her tendency to identify herself with the object of her love, she loves herself still more. Her narcissism, which is more finely shaded, can stop at the resemblance of the subjects. Feminine intuition is one of the results of this tendency to identification. Narcissism is a defense against two other tendencies, the passivity which delivers her as object to man's active sexual influence, and masochism.

Passivity is inherent in the whole of her reproductive functions and in her aptitude to conform with the rhythm of masculine sexuality. It should not be taken as pure inertia, but as "activity directed inward."

Woman's aggressiveness, like her activity, is turned inward, and becomes *masochism*. From beginning to end, from defloration to childbirth, the reproductive function "requires acceptance of a certain suffering." Feminine masochism is the ability to find pleasure in this suffering which is inseparable from love. Woman's desire to love may easily turn into a desire to be loved (passivity), and this is tantamount to the desire to experience the torments of love (masochism).

According to the combinations and degrees of integration of these three factors, we will have two types of woman who are equally "feminine" in that they possess the components of femaleness. The passive feminine woman and the active feminine woman are designated by the difference in balance of these three factors.

The "passive" woman is characterized "by a proneness to identi-

[1] Helene Deutsch, *The Psychology of Women*, 2 vols. (New York: Grune & Stratton, 1944).

fication, openness to influences, masochistic renunciation in favor of another." This passivity is guarded by narcissism which protects her against masculine demands, thereby making her more fascinating and mysterious.

The "active" woman is one who feels more strongly about womanly activities directed inward, toward the life of the home, the building and care of the "family nest." In such activity her masochism tends to take on a moral color. Narcissism reinforces her in her demands that she be accorded respect, and in her search for strength of character and personality in those she loves.

These two specifically feminine types of woman find their fulfillment in real or sublimated motherhood.

But we also find the "virilized" woman, whose aggressive tendencies are less inhibited and whose activities are directed outward, the woman whose masculinity complex is more or less virulent. This complex produces domineering mothers as easily as women of action.

Helene Deutsch's books, particularly her essay on woman's sexuality,* are developments of the Freudian analyses:

> There are three large categories of women who have reacted differently to the decisive trauma of the little girl's discovery of difference between the sexes. One type of woman early replace penis envy by a desire for children and these have become real women—normal, vaginal and maternal. Others have given up competition with men because, feeling that their equipment is too unequal, they have renounced all objective sexuality and find psychic and social realization in the human species—something that can be observed in the bee-workers or in the ant hill. Finally, there are others who, in spite of their refusal to accept reality and in fact their denial of it, hold on to that psychic and organic virility which every woman possesses and which is a complex of virility and clitoris.[2]

* *Psychoanalyse der weiblichen Sexualfunktionen* (Vienna: Internat. Psychoanal. Verlag, 1925).—*Trans.*

[2] Marie Bonaparte, "De la sexualité de la femme," *Revue Française de Psychanalyse*, I (1949), p. 1.

SIGNIFICANCE OF PSYCHOANALYTICAL DIFFERENTIATION

We must not pause to ask if elaborating a thesis on female psychology is "activity directed inward" for a woman. Helene Deutsch congeals the Freudian thesis and hardens mechanisms into universal stereotypes. Nor shall we choose a subtle method which would allow us to fit every genesis into an all-inclusive analysis. The first discernible facets of innumerable possible future developments of personality are here congealed into definitive schemas. From genesis, the dawn of an indescribable day, one descends into the narrow passages of a prison.

In this perspective, the professional activity of numerous women today is contrary to their deeper "nature." In France, for instance, for many years now one out of three women has been a worker. Thus for each two men there exists one woman whose activity is "turned to the outer world" in the same way as theirs. Must we subtract these 6,500,000 women from the total female population; must we, by a new and simple calculation, estimate the proportion of women condemned to neurosis by modern society?[3] No doubt a certain number of men and women are quick to blame their hardships on the industrial age and the loss of the interplay with nature that existed in agrarian cultures. Unfortunately, we must tell them that the reverse is true, that neuroses are more frequent among women who remain in the home. More than one in three of these women (36 per cent) suffer from mental illnesses.[4] This figure does not include the feeble-minded or those floundering in vice and poverty.

The question asked by Dr. Lebovici remains to be answered: "Notions of woman's masochism, woman's passivity, and phallic envy on the part of the woman should not be discarded. There is, however, reason to ask whether they have not been produced

---

[3] The census of 1962 gives 6,489,000 women and 12,467,000 men as making up the total French working population.

[4] *Courrier de l'UNESCO* (May 1959). Genevieve Texier, in "Virilité et Feminité, pseudo-concepts" (*La Nef* [January–March 1961], p. 89) presents a similar argument.

by our culture or whether, on the contrary, they express the biological and psychological *status* of woman."[5]

Can these conceptual constructions be interpreted as the fixed "nature" of the social roles and psychological influences of family organization as found in agrarian civilizations, or do they inevitably describe woman's unchangeable characteristics? The woman forms the heart of the family, the husband is head of the home—these things are repeated in more modern terms. It cannot be denied that this type of family has created admirable homes where men and women have found or could have found happiness. It is no less certain that agricultural civilization is fading into the past.

Psychoanalysis opportunely recalls that sexuality is a genesis. It is a history which defines what is masculine and what is feminine or, more simply, human; it shows that every action and all modes of conduct cannot be defined in themselves, that they are links between the past and the future. There is a more profound meaning in the question which cuts across this whole history in which a person fashions himself and arrives at self-knowledge: How is experience unified in the integration of the ego? In what way has this integration been colored by maleness or femaleness? By its concepts, its structures, and its methods psychoanalysis enables us better to grasp and express the dynamic continuity of personal integration in the midst of conflicts; when it speaks of repression, fixation, suppression, defense, retrogression, perversion, sublimation, it is dealing with universal mechanisms, with structures of personal time.

The structures are universal but the structured object is not. Is there even an object? There is no background; it is a genesis that is structured, not a "nature." We know that Malinowski was the first to criticize the Oedipus complex. As hatred of the father, the so-called universality of this complex is not in keeping with cultural pluralism. Attachments and conflicts both vary with family structure. For example, among the Trobriand Islanders studied by Malinowski the child belongs to his mother's family and tribe; the child inherits the social position of his mother's

[5] *Esprit* (November 1960), p. 1684.

brother, and hatred and rivalry are transferred to the person of this uncle. In similar manner, it can happen that incestuous feelings are transferred from mother to sister. What is universal is the child's ambivalent attitude toward the person who has a certain status, namely, toward the one in his family who personifies authority and discipline. This childish attitude has a history which is structured in accord with the universal mechanisms of psychoanalysis.[6] Further, it is more than likely that this interpretation of psychoanalysis is in keeping with the most profound and original insights of Sigmund Freud himself.

What we should retain of psychoanalysis, rather than Helene Deutsch's classifications, is its lesson that femaleness and maleness are the result of two geneses. And the deep animality, the sexual instinct will only be perceived through and beyond this human genesis. In man, sex is a historical process; and the results of this history, which it is permissible to classify, vary according to cultures. Only if they are reclassified and compared according to period and customs will a comparison of this kind be of service to anthropology. But history and genesis obey universal mechanisms.

Some years ago an attempt was made to establish theories about symbols in some obscure zone and then to supply it with a content; people were inclined to believe that this content differed for man and woman, and for such banal reasons as the symbolic transposition of physiological organs. What is in doubt today is the very existence of such a content; there certainly is a genesis of man and woman, but is not certain that this genesis presupposes a definite background. The significance of symbols, whether they be sexual or other, is a matter of "position," according to Lévi-Strauss. The significance attached to a symbolic term results from a kind of combining function which this term is called upon to play in a given cultural context; it varies with the culture. The symbolic significance remains valid, outside the affirmed positions of structuralism.

The sexed body, the malleable avatar of a personal condition, takes on a definite direction as masculine or feminine in a given

6 Cf. Mikel Dufrenne, *La Personnalité de base* (Paris: P.U.F., 1953), pp. 78 ff.

culture, that is, in a relational whole, which is more or less like a field of force in which the elements can be isolated and changed only according to given laws, and by finding new direction in a new structured whole. This whole varies as do relationships and functions in the field of force. The male-female relationship is a genesis of this order and cannot be specified once and for all, but must be explained relative to a given culture.

Aggressive, masochistic, and exhibitionist tendencies are universal, of course, and it is easy to transfer them from the symbolization in which they are veiled to conscious eroticism. It is much more hazardous to specify them according to sexual differentiation. All these tendencies have a history from which they can be separated only through a useless abstraction made in the delusion that it will yield a more precise definition.

Still more subtly, sexuality is by its inevitably relational character inseparable from human growth and genesis. It is this genesis itself under a particular but fundamental aspect. As a history that begins before birth, sexuality is something wholly different from a definitive and definable characteristic: we must henceforth grasp this history in the very reciprocity of the sexes.

CHAPTER FIVE

Femininity as Subjection

Simone de Beauvoir also sees history as defining masculinity and femininity, but it is exclusively the history of economic and social relations. Her book is valuable mainly for its critical examination of her subject, and for the questions it raises concerning many things hitherto too easily taken for granted.[1] Despite the sometimes tiresome insistence on descriptions in Book II, her critique is all to the good—the critique, not necessarily its underlying thesis. This critique is radical, because she holds that opposition and distinction between masculine and feminine have no more specific meaning, at least for today, than those between "lord" and "vassal," and should be completely abolished.

WOMAN WITHIN THE MASTER-SLAVE DIALECTIC

Femininity, so called, is for Simone de Beauvoir a situation existing within a given culture, nothing more. Femininity (or what is usually called femininity) cannot be finally determined by biological data or some mysterious feminine essence—Christian mythology, or romanticism, or simply the prejudices of a social class. The distinction results from a factual situation in the economic order: man's predominance in the world through centuries of history. "All of the history of women has been made by men."[2] The sole source of our present definition of the feminine character is the situation of women in economic and social relations, which

[1] *The Second Sex* (New York: Alfred A. Knopf, 1953; paperback, New York: Bantam Books, 1961).
[2] *Ibid.* (Bantam), p. 118.

cuts women off from any independence or truly personal mode of life.

There is no real distinction between the sexes on the personal level; their physiological roles are different, but the person is sexually neutral. In the man-woman conflict we confront a special instance of the unique master-slave dialectic. Women should be counted among the oppressed, the proletariat; women form a class of human beings who are alienated and frustrated, exploited in their work like the other exploited classes. For thousands of years man's domination has made woman what she is, and woman has in the end been satisfied with the position created for her, at least to the point of accepting it in the same way a peasant of the Middle Ages might have considered his serfdom as a condition ordained by natural law. "The privileged place held by men in economic life, their social usefulness, the prestige of marriage, the value of masculine backing, all this makes women wish ardently to please men. Women are still, for the most part, in a state of subjection. It follows that woman sees herself and makes her choices not in accordance with her true nature, but as man defines her."[3]

Woman's reactions to her situation as member of an exploited class have often been ineffectual and confused. But, as in other such cases, the exploiters themselves have been divided. Men have frequently been known to exploit feminist organizations for their own political ends. As alienated individuals, women have most often been content to seek refuge either in eroticism, or mysticism, or in a sublimation of the "eternal feminine."

It was man who created the myth of the eternal feminine—but here we must beware, for in this myth woman was set up as an ideal, an ideal for man. In the eternal feminine the woman appears essentially as the Other, the ultimate symbol of incompleteness. It is amazing that the myth of the eternal feminine has so long remained static, fated to immobilize and stabilize woman's condition of subjection. This situation alienates her further, or rather becomes "a point of spiritual honor."

It would be senseless to deny biological differences, but we must

[3] *Ibid.*, pp. 127–28.

seriously doubt that they determine personality; they are simply conditions, among others, of existence. Concluding her reply to a questionnaire sent out by the review *La Nef*, Simone de Beauvoir argues as follows against an earlier article in the same review:

> And "the little difference"? The physiological data will remain in any case, as M. d'Ormesson points out. We know, however, that with the progress of automation, the question of physical strength is losing its importance; as for resistance and skill, women have enough of these and to spare. A well-organized economy could easily make provision for leave during pregnancies; if arranged and agreed to, neither production nor the woman worker would suffer. We still have to deal with laws, which according to M. d'Ormesson prescribes the specific character of woman's destiny. Let us reassure him. With good morale and good health, the majority of women can manage very well. It is masculine mythology that points out the afflicting and somehow shameful signs of our weakness; were men submitted to it, they would consider the monthly donation of their blood as something superbly virile; while a woman remains the economically underdeveloped sex, any feature particular to masculinity symbolizes only superiority in the eyes of the male."[4]

And what has she to say of the "vocation for motherhood" which tradition assigns to feminine physiology and character—that never-ceasing and imperative call to maternity which Adrienne Sahuqué earlier described as "gynecological intimidation"? On this point Simone de Beauvoir writes: "And the child? He demands the constant attention of his mother; he complains: 'The lady next door stays home all day . . . why do you have to go to work? Because papa doesn't make enough money?' We forget that with a child questions such as these are not spontaneous and naïve; they are not natural, but are suggested by what he hears around him; no one is more conformist than he; it is the anomaly of the situation that upsets him; he would accept it without demur if everyone took it for granted."

These are some of the principal points of the thesis Simone de Beauvoir seeks to prove in diverse and converging ways—by

[4] Simone de Beauvoir, "La Condition féminine," special number of *La Nef* on "Woman" and "Love" (January-March 1961), p. 126.

sociology, by history, and even by literary criticism, since literature reflects man's image of womanhood.

At the base of this radical negation of the difference between
men and women on the strictly human plane, and of the denial
that biological differences could have repercussions on the economic and social plane, we find the theses of Jean-Paul Sartre, for
whom human nature or indeed any nature, as such does not exist.
How can sexuality influence economics if economics comes first?
Man is pure possibility, he is only what he does, he identifies
himself with his existential project—it is this project that defines
him, whether he be man or woman. There is no human datum, no
point of departure; man is fundamentally a pure potential; one is
not born man or woman, one becomes one or the other. Thus there
is no reason to seek a natural basis for the distinction between
men and women; it is purely a matter of sociological conditioning.

Since the man-woman struggle brings alienation, how should one
go about abolishing it?

First, woman must become aware that she is exploited (and
at the same time of the truth of Sartre), and must reject everything
that falsely appears as a natural datum while in fact it is only the
tradition of slavery. Through such awareness, woman will cease to
be bound by so-called feminine values; she will be what she does
and what she makes of herself; fundamentally she is only a
project.

She must not permit this project of *being* to be degraded into a
project of *having*. She must reject all measures of semiliberation.
It matters little that new careers are being opened to women, here
we are still in the domain of having. She continues to be the
prisoner of a pseudonature, of pseudofemininity. Woman will
remain a slave so long as she must be married in order to gain any
real position in social life. Her true vocation cannot be motherhood—real or sublimated; certainly no one dreams of assigning
paternity to man as his supreme vocation. The same existential
project defines both man and woman.

Real liberation can be achieved only in a socialist world, that is,
a world where man, finally free of nature, will depend on nothing
other than his labor. Within this society he will at last conform

to his fundamental reality, in his pure capacity as *homo faber* to transform nature and remake himself.

> In order for woman to attain that professional equality on which all else depends, there must be work for all; this implies a great increase of worldly prosperity and the rationalization of production on a universal scale. It is pointless to speculate about the morrows of our prehistory. What is certain is that progress toward abundance and reason can come about only through the overthrow of our present productive system. If women are not satisfied with finding individual solutions for their problem, they must fight on the side of those men who want to hasten this overthrow.[5]

HOW IS LOVE POSSIBLE?

Simone de Beauvoir's thesis is a radical critique which removes all romanticism from femininity. And it is true that there is a whole series of false sublimations, a veritable mythology based on social factors. But the position she adopts assumes the absence of all true community between man and woman, and the impossibility of communion between them. There is not and cannot be a successful unity in the manner of a "Thou-and-I" relation. Each man and each woman is an island in the ocean, without oars or sails, open to the high seas but nonetheless the only center of reference. And if the center is defined by nothing other than this openness, love can be conceived only in the mode of having, of possession. By this very fact all love is doomed to failure, for it makes the other an object.

Yet for this being, based on nothingness, it is also impossible not to search beyond himself for that help, support, and comforting response which is always outside of him. This is the fragility of a project which can be defined only by separation, or ecstacy, which leads us to dream of a subject who would no longer be a perpetual projection, but a harmony, a god. Love is of a kind with that dynamism which creates the gods. More fragile and less suspect because of the factitiousness of the body in which the sexual need is rooted, the project of loving has for its purpose the welfare

[5] De Beauvoir, "La Condition féminine," p. 127.

of my own factitiousness and individuality. My individual existence will take on importance to the degree that I succeed in having it accepted by another. My own existence, that hazardous datum, will be restored to me by another for whom it has become necessary; the other will make my contingency his own end. Then my existence will be justified, I will have reason to live, I will be saved from meaninglessness.

The happiness which is to be realized at the attainable height of love is precarious and unstable; although certainly not illusory, it is destructible and transitory. Here is a description of the "joy of love": "Whereas we felt ourselves 'de trop' we now feel that our existence is taken up and willed even in its tiniest details by an absolute freedom which at the same time our existence conditions and which we ourselves will with our freedom. This is the basis for the joy of love, when there is joy: we feel that our existence is justified."[6]

Then, as Simone de Beauvoir stresses, "The verbs *to give* and *to receive* exchange meanings; joy is gratitude, pleasure is affection. Under a concrete and carnal form there is mutual recognition of the ego and of the other in the keenest awareness of the other and of the ego. . . . What is required for such harmony is not refinement in technique, but rather, on the foundation of the moment's erotic charm, a mutual generosity of body and soul."[7]

To arrive at this harmony and perpetuate it, to preserve anything as fragile as this in order to make myself loved, is to conquer the love of the other. This desire itself makes the harmony more fragile. Seeking to attract love is to risk its destruction. The strategy will be seduction, a campaign of expression by means of acts and words for the purpose of conquest, for what is at stake is the conquest of another's liberty. I must win for myself this indispensable and loving look; I must therefore incorporate my ego in this being who is seen, and identify myself with that being. In this identification with my objectivized expression, my project of conquest itself becomes expressive. In every project I use words and

[6] J.-P. Sartre, *Being and Nothingness* (New York: Philosophical Library, 1956), p. 371.
[7] *The Second Sex*, p. 377.

language; but I never know what I am signifying; in placing my whole ego in the expression of my project, I am forcing myself to be none else than a fascinating object. Thus I accede to magic; I identify myself insofar as I am able by means of whose power I am totally ignorant.

The project of loving is contradictory. It is contradictory in its purpose: to possess another's liberty as an object and at the same time to leave it free. There is contradiction at the heart of the project: the wish for the other's look to be free so that he will remain a subject, and at the same time the project to conquer that freedom. The contradiction is compounded if I want to be loved in return, and I must want it—to love is to want to be loved and for the other to want to be loved by me. This project is based on a reciprocity which tends toward unification and forces me to act on the freedom of the other; I desire to remain fascinating, unique, and irreplaceable as object and at the same time no longer to be this object. In the same act, I want to be both subject and object for the other and for the other to be both subject and object for me.

There can be only derisory compensations for the failure of love. One of the most frequent is masochism; I accept not to be a subject, and wish to be treated as a thing. On the other hand, instead of denying my ego, I can prefer the negation of the other. In unpremeditated form this is indifference; the other will be treated as a thing. When the other looks at me, I return a gaze of indifference, and the affirmation that the one before me is a subject collapses under my eyes. In more conscious form this indifference becomes impudence. Impudence presupposes bad faith and is not assumed with ease; it is impossible not to realize that just as I feel oppressed when someone stares at me blankly, I have oppressed the other in the same way. Another way out would be the complete reverse of love—hate, an attitude which is also reduction of a subject to an object, the same negation of a subject other than myself, but this time premeditated and intentional. The other is an object, I make him an object and consciously destroy him as subject.

The same destruction of my ego and of the other is expressed in sexual desire. Desire reduces the other to a mere response. The other has a desirable body; my attitude to the other has only to do with this body—a body which is not only an object of pleasure but a living and animated body that also radiates the spirit. I identify the other's freedom with this body and at the same time, the better to possess it, I identify myself with my own body, I engulf myself in my body. By a caress, I force myself to incarnate the other into my own flesh; and at the same time and with the same gesture that I caress the other I also caress myself. This endeavor to engulf the spirit in the flesh is a complicated process. The confrontation of two desires is nothing else than the encounter of two egos who become one and dissolve in the body.

Community is possible only on an entirely different basis. We must examine the origin of this sentiment of "we." Community arises only in a deep feeling of *Mitsein,* of "being-with." This presupposes an apprehension of the other in a different way than through an antagonistic glance, a sort of lateral awareness that may be likened to lateral sight. My awareness of myself as subject presupposes the other and awareness of the other; I am with, but I do not know with whom. It is through the look of another that I become aware of the feeling of belonging to a "marginal we," a feeling which this look has not engendered but which is presupposed on its part. The interaction of such looks is redoubled on the collective scale where, since love has no place, hate plays the more apparent role. The phenomena of collective hate produce renewed awareness of the "we-object." The feeling of the oppressed class is engendered merely by the way the capitalist looks at them. In its turn, the middle class, the bourgeoisie, has no class feeling until it has caused the rise of a class antagonistic to itself; the middle class sees itself as a "we-object" only when threatened with danger from the proletariat.

As for the "we-subject," this is always vague and difficult to grasp, and any comprehension of it must come in the form of a certain "we" subject. It grows out of work undertaken in common, as in the case of a work team or a cell of militant fighters for an ideology. At the lowest level is the complex feeling of being together which we find, for example, among those who march in a parade. There is nothing here to raise hopes for the intimacy of the Thou-and-I relation, that longed-for intimacy which is the sublimation of a desire which suppresses consciousness but at the same time can dazzle it with an imaginary mythology. Love, as the authentic confrontation of two subjects, remains forever impossible.[8] What remains is that fragile encounter in which the individual being finds a little reassurance and even a certain "joy of love."

SIMONE DE BEAUVOIR AND MARXISM

After Simone de Beauvoir it would be pointless to return to the naturalist's dreams of a biological destiny. On what, then, should the sexual differentiation be based, and how can we find in it any possibility of intimacy? It is impossible for us, even if we reject her thesis, not to accept a large part of Simone de Beauvoir's critique, or her revelations concerning the tremendous burden of history, of socioeconomic determinisms, of policies and ideologies. No reply to her is valid unless it takes into account her objections; we cannot remain naïvely content to perpetuate the ancient prejudices by continuing to canonize agrarian culture and family structure.

Simone de Beauvoir's position is similar to that of Marxism. Since man is man only by his work, woman will find herself only by integrating herself into the world of labor where her condition of slavery will come to an end. August Bebel and Friedrich Engels drew attention to woman's social situation, attributing it to history and dependence on the economic substructure.

But Karl Marx's own stand on this subject is extremely complex and does not permit a pure and simple definition of the relation of the sexes as an economic relation. For Marx, man's relation to woman remains of course a relation to nature, but the foundation of all relations to nature and is not based on some more vague and abstract approach. One of his essential texts, an apex it must be said, is found in the *Manuscripts of 1844.*

In the approach to *woman* as the spoil and handmaid of communal lust is expressed the infinite degradation in which man exists for himself, for the secret of this approach has its *unam-*

[8] Cf. A. Jeannière, "J.-P. Sartre et la liberté," in *Travaux et Jours*, No. 1, Beirut, April 1961).

biguous, decisive, *plain* and undisguised expression in the relation of *man to woman* and in the manner in which the *direct* and *natural* species relationship is conceived. This direct, natural, and necessary relation of person to person is the *relation of man to woman*. In this *natural* species relationship, man's relation to nature is immediately his relation to man, just as his relation to man is immediately his relation to nature—his own *natural* destination. In this relationship, therefore, is *sensuously manifested*, reduced to an observable *fact*, the extent to which the human essence has become nature to man, or to which nature to him has become the human essence of man. From this relationship one can therefore judge man's whole level of development. From the character of this relationship follows how much *man* as a *species of being*, as *man*, has come to be himself and to comprehend himself; the relation of man to woman is *the most natural* relation of human being to human being. It therefore reveals the extent to which the *human* essence in him has become a *natural* essence—the extent to which his *human nature* has come to be *nature to him*. In this relationship is revealed, too, the extent to which man's *need* has become a *human need*; the extent to which, therefore, the *other* person as a person has become for him a *need*—the extent to which he in his individual existence is at the same time a social being.[9]

For Marx defends the "love which first really teaches man to believe in the objective world outside himself, which not only makes man an object, but the object a man."[10] In fact, the man-woman relation is what makes it evident to him whether work really transcends the connection between animal and nature, and if it is human work, whether the connection with nature is humanized. For Karl Marx, sexuality is the very expression of human reality; even if nature does not create that reality, she is its basis and manifestation. The thought of the young Marx and Sartre are at opposite poles.

The importance of these texts lies in their emphasis on the similarities between the man-woman relation and the dual relation between man and man and between man and nature. Love

[9] *Economic and Philosophic Manuscripts of 1844*, Martin Milligan (New York: International Publishers, 1964), p. 134.

[10] K. Marx and F. Engels, *The Holy Family* (Moscow: Foreign Language Publishing House, 1956), p. 32.

appears in a twofold aspect—it unites two extremes. It is the attraction of the other as the other; namely, evidence of the opposition found in any conflict between man and the nature he transforms and humanizes, an opposition and attraction which defines the dual aspect of eroticism—the attraction of the individual and the urge of the species for survival. But love is still a relation to the other as man, a relation that defines the political dimension in its most immediate foundation. Further, in man's relation to woman, Marx makes the relation to the other as man (that is to say, the political relation) the very measure of humanization attained in relation to nature. The real and actually lived status of woman in a given society furnishes a concrete and observable criterion to establish this measure with certainty.

Although no doubt one must discount the accusations of "economism" brought against the later Karl Marx, the text of the *Manuscripts of 1844* remains an erratic block not really integrated into the system. In the disjunction between politics and economics under which we must live until the coming of a classless society, Karl Marx ordinarily considered woman's liberation as going hand in hand with the cooperation she is able to offer man in the further development of industrial production liberated from the constraint of private ownership.[11] Woman's alienation is therefore for him as for Simone de Beauvoir, a particular instance of oppression. Still, the Hegelian foundation of the Marxist dialectic quite frequently crops up and suggests the possibility of a union beyond the alternative of "bloody struggle or nothingness" which remains "the last word of social science."[12]

[11] Cf. G. Fessard, "Le Mystère de la Société," *Recherches de Science Religieuse* (April-May-June 1945), pp. 165–67.
[12] Karl Marx, *Morceaux choisies* (Paris: Gallimard), pp. 168–69.

CHAPTER SIX

Two Modes of Being-in-the-World?

P. J. J. Buytendijk's book *La Femme* is offered as a reply to *The Second Sex*.[1] As a matter of fact, the author tries to find new justification for the traditional values of femininity, while taking into account Simone de Beauvoir's criticisms and rejecting, as she does, a biological or psychological definition of the sexes. He also rejects the highly schematized conclusions which claim to rest in depth psychology. Psychological and anatomical structures have no significance and, at least so far as the first is concerned, no genesis, except in the global project of being human. Thus, in determining what is masculine and what is feminine, we cannot take into consideration either particular characteristics objectively verifiable or capacities proper to each sex because, however real these characteristics or capacities might be, they could very easily have been determined by cultural and social conditioning. We should not attribute determinative qualities to each of the sexes: believing that we are describing a characteristic, we build up a conditioning structure which it would perhaps be well to modify. Neither should we attribute to each sex a particular psychic capacity which, in the case of woman, would take us back to the fixed monolith of conditions referred to as "female nature." The cold logic and calculation of masculine concerns, woman's sensitivity or intuition—all this arises from fantasy, conservatism, or simply a catalogue of ideas handed down to us. In truly human undertakings, all those entered wholeheartedly, there is nothing that one sex can do better than the other, that is, if the other is not prevented by social structures.

[1] Paris: Desclée de Brouwer, 1954.

TWO MODES OF EXISTENCE: WORK AND CARE

Nevertheless, Buytendijk assures us, if men and women are able to devote themselves to the same specifically human tasks, they will carry them out in different ways, because each has his or her own mode of being-in-the-world.[2] There are two ways of being in the world, two ways of doing the same thing, one masculine and the other feminine. In this differentiation there is no question at all of a "nature" specifically distinguishing masculinity and femininity, but rather a freedom of choice starting with biological and social conditions. A certain interchange is therefore possible, desirable, and can moreover easily be observed. What is important is that the two modes of being, which are fundamental and complementary, continue to create interactions of mutual benefit. Both are necessary, and they cannot be fused into one. These two modes of being in the world are the mode of work and the mode of care.

The *masculine* mode of existence is the mode of *work*: to know and transform nature for a given purpose. Man's fundamental experience is the resistance of the world, leading him to adopt an attitude in which a concrete sense of the necessities of a situation is joined to a sense of domination, a sense for adapting the means to the end.

The *feminine* mode of existence is *care*. This is not worried preoccupation or anxiety, but devotedness, the ability to bring tranquility and relaxation, in other words, what one would call the act of taking care. It is a certain way of taking care, of something or someone, carried to its perfection, thereby becoming a *mode of being near* to someone or something. "Existence . . . in the mode of coexistence." Woman's fundamental experience is the value of beings and the discovery, preservation, and engendering of these values.

In the sense woman will be more altruistic than man; not by nature but because her manner of being disposes her to the encounter with the other and leads her to remain with him. Care does not reach its full measure unless a human being is made its object; it is the act of being present in the mode of intimacy, the

[2] *Ibid.*, p. 329.

"we" of the one who cares and the one for whom one cares.

Hence care is the altruism that leads to authentic interiorness, interiorness not enclosed within itself or in a dream, but fruitful. At the same time as it places itself close to the other, care obliges one to remain close to oneself. The passionate life does not consist in struggle and expansion, but in immanence and interiorness. In this way woman will remain close to herself and live her interior life intensely; she will at the same time have care for her own corporeality, the sense of charm in her very presence.

All the "ladies of yesteryear" were quick to acquiesce in a mode of existence so in keeping with their own—the ladies of poem and song: the chatelaine at the tower window, the infanta caressing the male gazelle, the princess of the symbolic unicorn, all the innumerable weaving Penelopes with their minds on some Ulysses. To these are added the ladies of the "Book of Reasons," the guardians of vast domains, alike in their active and gentle melancholy; also the ladies of the "Book of Hours," so often praised for their knowledge of womanly being. All these, including the adventuress with the heart of gold, are summoned up on condition that they knew how to enter the lists in the mode of care and with "feminine" weapons. This all-too-perfect correspondence with the stereotypes of the past necessarily engenders a certain apprehension. Does the truth of our day so closely resemble these literary images?

Buytendijk replies that the feminine mode of existence is today of particular value, because of all the openhandedness and disinterestedness it presupposes, because it is altercentric, and finally because there emerges with it an entire ethic which is more precious than ever before.

The role and importance of the feminine mode of existence are increased in our present civilization, a civilization of work and hence masculine, and overly preoccupied with results and abstract rationality, with organization and efficiency. Woman brings to it her own values of disinterested presence and active openhandedness and, accordingly, of luxury and beauty. In the mode of work, everything is finalized, whereas care is the domain of the openhanded.

Care is altercentric. It is expressed in the giving of self, in the tenderness inspired by the frailty, gentleness, and weakness of the one for whom care is felt—it flowers in the vocation to maternity.

For Buytendijk, this vocation to motherhood is not prescribed or determined a priori by biology or by a certain "feminine nature," but is the end of existential analysis. The maternal vocation is the consequence of a mode of being, a free and fundamental choice among determinisms, not the result of sublimation of instinct or a destiny. A woman does not need to have children to be motherly, but we cannot fail to see how the feminine mode of existence in the world, namely care, presupposes presence to the other, constant presence to the other, all the more intense and radiant in proportion to the other's frailty—care reaches its peak in the care of a mother for her child.

It is possible for a woman to reveal this same maternal solicitude for a man; in receiving and giving, she can reveal toward him the same maternal manner of having care of the other without at the same time stifling his energies. On the contrary, she can arouse them and, in receiving and giving, reawaken in man the pristine energies of a never-forgotten childhood.

These modes of being unfold in two contrasting ethics. "The authentically masculine or feminine being is a form of spiritual being. . . . Manliness is apparent in the ethic which combines duty, obedience, courage, effort, and the will to achieve an aim. Woman's existence, because of her care for others, attests to a moral existence composed of disinterested love and self-renunciation." This ethic is all the more necessary today because "if we reduce a man's existence to work without his ethic of duty being anchored to love, this existence would be no more than constant anxiety, incessant change from one aim to another, from one subject to another, a restless existence in which day after day is spent in escaping from himself and escaping from reality."[3]

Thus, in the mode of work, the world is lived in an ethic of duty, and the moral references of the man of action will be by choice: will, power, duty, efficiency. In the mode of care, the world is lived in an ethic of love and devotedness, made up of confidence, attentiveness, respect and submission, and fruitfulness.

[3] *Ibid.*, p. 336.

THE RELIGIOUS AURA

Buytendijk's thesis can be illustrated by an example from Paul Claudel, and by a reading of Claudel's *Satin Slipper*. "Woman brings the desert to man," Claudel wrote. She brings him the desert in the sense that she closes off to him the road of action in order to teach him beauty, generosity, disinterestedness. Donna Prouhèze is more precious to Rodrigues than America; there is something more important than the world to conquer and unite, but Prouhèze herself cannot be conquered. She is more precious than the mirage of Eldorado, but she will not be possessed. Possessing her, Rodrigues would perhaps have rediscovered his conquering instincts, he could have conquered Prouhèze, but Prouhèze has taught him about the desert, she has brought Rodrigues' childhood to life and with it the sense of interior enlivenment, a taste for things inaccessible to "work," simply for the reason that they are more human. In his voyages, his struggles, in his sway of power, he had come into collision with the harshness of things and laws—with organization, objects, even with the inhuman; in meeting Prouhèze he discovers a human being from whom he cannot escape, nor can he triumph over her.

In the desert, silence is linked to the deep interiorness of "care." Woman is perfection in being, in a certain mode of being; she can realize herself only in silence and in meditation—this is not to say that she is unable to act and even to initiate action to the same extent as man. So Prouhèze rules in Mogador while Rodrigues commands in the New Indies. But she does not dominate Mogador in Rodrigues' way, and above all she does not dominate the Moor whom she eventually marries. If she is the mistress of Mogador, it is by marshaling all her interior forces, by imposing her presence. She commands in the mode of care.

This example allows us to carry the existential analysis beyond Buytendijk and to bring out the religious aura that surrounds these classical analyses. At the same time as she brings the desert, the woman brings God. Prouhèze says to the Angel: "Yes, I am able to bring God to him." Only presence in the mode of care evokes the more fundamental perfection of the Presence. "The woman who is grace." And carnal grace itself is made up of these qualities: the gift of repose, the gift of self, under the charm of silence, in the burning desert of intimacy.

The first of the *Five Great Odes* shows us woman as the image of divine grace—or rather, through her grace appears, is made manifest. This is a traditional image. In Scripture the woman is the image of Wisdom who is the Word. An analysis along the lines we have just suggested could be based on Scripture; not only passages and images but anecdotes are plentiful. The encounter of David and Abigail, for example, a pastoral story the outline of which could easily be shifted to a modern novel. Intelligent and beautiful, Abigail, the neglected wife, flowered at the side of her wretched husband. His name was Nabal, that is "the Boor," and he came into violent conflict with David, a rebel fellah wandering about with his flock. Abigail went out to meet David armed with her own weapons. At this meeting she taught him wisdom and revealed to him a dimension of life he had not known. Nabal dying shortly thereafter, Abigail departed with a David just as pugnacious as before but become more human; she had taught him what it is to be a man.[4]

Moreover when the silent being attains perfection, as with the Blessed Virgin, she gives God to man, gives him the fullness of humanity with the Man-God. Thus Mary was to be, in the words of Paul Claudel, "the sacrament of God's maternal tenderness."

It is necessary to make reference to this religious aura, because the reason that many refuse to face the problem of woman's actual evolution is because they are taking into account both the amplitude and duration of traditional images and the effects of their rapid and continuous disintegration.

SEXUAL CATEGORIES INDEPENDENT OF SEX!

It is most difficult, even on the symbolic level, to enter on a study of sexual anthropology or its equivalent based on masculine and feminine distinctions in the Bible. If God is the Bridegroom,

[4] I Sam., 25:2–44.

the people of God, including man, are the Bride. And a member of the faithful is always the spouse (feminine), even according to St. John of the Cross. The Word, the Wisdom of God, is sometimes masculine, sometimes feminine. God himself is always masculine, sometimes the spouse and sometimes the father; but it also happens that he likens himself to the mother who caresses the little children at her knee, or, as we read in Revelation, who "wipes away the tears from their eyes"—the description, it would seem, of a maternal action on God's part. It would no doubt be possible and interesting to deduce the complex logic of these interchangeable relations and functions, but probably quite vain to draw fixed sexual characteristics from them in order to define temperaments or manners of being.

On the level of existential analysis, Buytendijk provides an entering wedge for criticism of his own theories, but he fails to draw the final conclusions. In the passage quoted above in which he defines manliness, we omitted the parenthetical sentence in which he declares that such manliness could easily pertain to an individual of the feminine sex. In fact, to constitute truly and fully a human being, one must achieve the two projects within one self—namely, the projects of living both in the mode of work and the mode of care. Or, to exhaust however humbly the field of ordinary possibility, one must find a different equilibrium for each. Male and female elements are to be found in each of us, man or woman. But in affirming, as Buytendijk does, that all feminine characteristics can be found in a man and that all masculine characteristics can legitimately be shown by a woman, does he not relativize his analysis to the point of having it fail of its purpose? Even the maternal character, he asserts, can be independent of the sexual body. Thus masculinity and femininity become independent of the sex of individuals both in religious symbolism and in existential anthropology.

Well then, if it is legitimate to distinguish two modes of being, why separate them? Above all, why separate them in order to give them a sexual application? Again, why use this explanation to reinforce and perpetuate the oppressive function of the agrarian images of woman? Implicitly, in fact, Buytendijk ends up with the opposite of what he wanted to prove—namely, that the subject is neutral. Does not everything finally depend on the project of being one achieves, and which leads one to live at times in the mode of care within an ethic of love, at other times in the mode of work within the ethic of duty? Although independent of sex, one of these projects is arbitrarily called feminine, the other masculine, whereas each man and each woman must find a balance between these two modes of being, a balance which has little to do with sex. Is it not dangerous to divide these modes of existence between the two sexes and to universalize the traditional images handed down to us by certain cultures? Do we not run the risk of condemning individuals to an alienating bias?

Actually, masculine and feminine become more flexible as categories, but without any possibility of individual or collective application, either definitive or even definite. This is a convenient classification of two modes of being in relation to one's ego, to nature, to others, and even to God. Buytendijk, who seems perfectly aware of this, ends with references to the studies and reports of Margaret Mead. The already outdated investigations of this ethnologist (1932–33) reveal the sexual categories of three primitive tribes in New Guinea in geographical proximity to each other.[5]

"Whereas the Arapesh have standardized the personality of both men and women in a mould that, out of our traditional bias, we should describe as maternal, womanly, unmasculine, the Mundugumor have gone to the opposite extreme and, again ignoring sex as a basis for the establishment of personality differences, have standardized the behavior of both men and women as actively masculine, virile, and without any of the softness and mellowing characteristics that we are accustomed to believe are inalienably feminine."[6]

Among the Tchambuli, the women are robust and practical; they have a sense of organization and are sexually aggressive. The men are passive, emotional, coquettish; they like to chat endlessly, and their preferred occupations are of the artistic order—dancing and painting. They are easily offended and show the resentment

[5] Margaret Mead, *From the South Seas: Studies of Adolescence and Sex in Primitive Societies* (New York: William Morrow & Co., 1939).

[6] *Ibid.*, Pt. 3, p. 165.

of persons who feel themselves weak and isolated. The women treat them like grown-up children. Nevertheless, this society is of the patrilineal type, but "the actual dominance of the woman is far more real than the structural position of the men."[7] Margaret Mead writes further: "While there is reason to believe that not every Tchambuli woman is born with a dominating, organizing, administrative temperament, actively sexed and willing to initiate sex-relations, possessive, definite, robust, practical and impersonal in outlook, still most Tchambuli girls grow up to display these traits. And while there is definite evidence to show that all Tchambuli men are not, by native endowment, the delicate, responsive actors of a play staged for the women's benefit, still most Tchambuli boys manifest this coquettish play-acting personality most of the time."[8]

Buytendijk is perfectly aware of all this, so we will end our chapter with a quotation from his book which greatly relativizes his own position:

One tribe in the Philippines thinks that no man can keep a secret. The Manus say that only men enjoy playing with babies; the Todas that domestic work is too sacred to be entrusted to women. The Arapesh insist that women's heads are stronger than men's. These conceptions are important factors, for they determine the conceptions of the society. But here is an excellent example of the effect of a generally accepted opinion. The Mundugumor say that a child born with the umbilical cord around his throat is destined to become an artist—that is, a painter. The result is that one who is not born in this way will be timid, lacking in self-confidence and will acquire no great skill! So-called masculine or feminine characteristics are engendered in the same manner.

If we take the trouble to consider with humor and good sense what is accepted in our society as masculine or feminine, we will have no difficulty in discovering distinctions similar to those found among the Mundugumor.[9]

Up to this point we have merely highlighted along with Buytendijk the numerous facts that contradict the results of his

---

[7] *Ibid.*, p. 271.
[8] *Ibid.*, p. 288.
[9] Buytendijk, *op. cit.*, p. 342.

analysis, or at least strip it of meaning by making it independent of the man-woman differentiation which it was his intention to explain. We must now take a more basic approach to his thesis. Is it possible to replace nature-culture oppositions by fixed modes of being characterizing transition from one to the other? Is it even possible to characterize a nature-culture opposition beyond the interchangeable relations embedded in praxis, to go back to determinable sources? Are there two ways of "coming of age" in a culture —one masculine, the other feminine—which if they do not determine characteristics at least determine more than two ways of living, or modes of being?

CHAPTER SEVEN

Corporeal Dynamism

The modes of appearing are in constant interaction with the modes of being. How to hold our own before others is the problem, for the complicated interplays of social life interfere with plans that have seemed completely autonomous. To be and to appear: the two are one and the same way of knowing ourselves and of finding our place in the world. We cannot be otherwise than with others, known and unknown—looking and being looked at.

Buytendijk rightly stresses the bonds between appearing and corporeality. My body is my being-in-the-world, my state in the world; beginning with this fundamental state, I manifest myself as I create myself in daily practice. Thus we can agree with Buytendijk in calling the modes of appearing "corporeal dynamism" without, however, drawing the same conclusions.[1]

Neither shall we start out with the body-object—we know already that this leads to an impasse—but with a living body, a body such as my own, studied dynamically in its genesis. We shall start with the idea I have of my body as well as with the body as it escapes me, start with corporeality itself without seeking the im-

[1] P. J. J. Buytendijk, *op. cit.*, pp. 290 ff. In the foreword to his book he sums up his reasoning as follows: We believe we can define the world of woman as the *world of care*, the world of men as that of *work*. The origin of these worlds is revealed in the first experiences of a small child: the girl forms a world of qualities in conforming herself to them; the boy a world of obstacles in resisting them. In the first case dynamism is characterized primarily by adaptation, in the second by tension and aggressiveness." The difficulty here is to agree that dynamism, namely the structure of behavior, is "corporeally determined." Determinations are highly varied and not always decisive.

possible dichotomy between object and subject. We will place ourselves in the human world to study the genesis of corporeality. For if, to begin with, there is no basically unchangeable constant to limit the free subject individually, a dangerous convergence of determinisms nevertheless constitutes itself as a situation, as a datum at once brutal and fluid; I am born with my freedom challenged by all that is other, and seems bent on imposing itself on me, but in the name of necessity.

Such a conflict with nature, the given and the environment, focuses the attention of each man and each woman on his body at the same time as it leads him to an understanding of his bodily condition and that of the other as masculine and feminine. We are thus led back to the perpetual and fundamental problem of the transition from biological irrationality to social rationality.

THE BODY AS DIALECTICAL REALITY

There is the body as a mass of chemical components in interaction, the body as dialectic of living being and its biological milieu, and the body as the dialectic of social subject and his group; even all our habits are an impalpable body for the ego of each moment. Each of these stages is the soul of the preceding stage, the body of the subsequent stage. The body in general is an ensemble of beaten paths, of powers already constituted; the body is the acquired dialectical soil upon which a higher "formation" is accomplished, and the soul is the meaning that is then established."[2]

The body is not a reality definable once and for all; like the mind, it escapes from the conceptual net in which we seek to trap it. What exists is the very tension of the body-mind dialogue; this tension is man himself. Our corporeality is the genesis; we can distinguish stages but cannot definitively determine a step forward. The reciprocity of male and female places us outside the determinations of the living being *qua* living being, and into a dialectic of the group and the individual subject. In this dialectic the sexed body appears as one conditioning among many others, a

[2] M. Merleau-Ponty, *The Structure of Behavior* (Boston: Beacon Press, 1942), p. 210.

conditioning itself the culmination of a genesis. We are dealing with one of the threads in an immense skein of relationships interwoven on different levels, and the relational whole alone is concrete and mobile. In this inexhaustible reality of the human world from which I may escape only in my dreams, each individual appears as an abstract element, but also as a mediator. It is, in fact, in this individuality assured by the very hazards of his body that each human being discovers the real totality of his own flesh which is the world. The external nature from which man arises, from which he must withdraw in order to rediscover his own nature, has already become and is daily becoming more and more "the vast inorganic body of humanity."[3]

If there are planes and levels, there also is a unity of human reality, and this unity is often called by the ambiguous word *nature*. This unity must not be understood only in the strict and definitive logic of a human world that is static, but as the unity of a mobile genesis in which man distinguishes himself not only by self-knowledge but as an inseparable element of that external nature which he knows only in making it other, in transforming and humanizing it. There can be no division into objectivity and subjectivity; there exists only their inseparable unity in human *praxis*.

It has been necessary to refer to these classic generalities because the sexed body is itself only one fundamental element of the mode of living of our situation in the world. A whole range of undefined differences and gradations opens before us in attitudes we take toward this body as a datum.

SEXUALITY AND FREEDOM

The differentiation between masculine and feminine specific to mankind is lived in the mode of a confrontation; it is a relation. When the male-female relationship, fundamental for the species, is objectified in the differentiation of masculine and feminine, it affects the individual to the core of his personal autonomy; but here we face a social phenomenon existing within a given culture.

[3] Cf. Karl Marx, *Economic and Social Manuscripts of 1844, op. cit.*, p. 112.

This transposition from the species to the person is the encounter of man and woman only as it takes place within the limits of a culture, a language, traditions, a world of communications. In this encounter the body plays a fundamental role provided it is accepted as a human body, not as a simple physicochemical composite or the combination of a certain number of biological functions. In the man-woman relation the sexed body is no doubt a datum, an object of chance, but it is already endowed with meaning.

Thus we must study the encounter itself, and not try to isolate two characters that existed before their confrontation. In this sense, the content of pseudo concepts of masculinity and femininity is the function of a culture: such concepts flow from the encounter to the interior of the human world; it is the encounter that establishes them and not the other way around. We should not be surprised to find that human love is not purely and simply in continuity with the biological factor, or that the human spirit is not simply the flower that blossoms at the summit of an organism, at the peak of an evolution; but that it is the true birth of an entirely new spiritual world, such that the very nature from which it springs is here laid open to question.

The biological factor has no meaning nor being (because it is modified according to its meaning) except through culture. By itself it is undetermined and almost inactive; alone it seems incapable of exercising a determinism except when cosmic or social circumstances clash with it too violently. Only in apocalyptic epochs, Shérif observes, during famines or wars, is the urgency of physical needs fully revealed, and necessity seizes the individual by the throat. Just so, when a culture takes no account of age or sex— when, for example, children are compelled to do the work of adults, or the older children are charged with duties belonging properly to a mother—this culture will suffer a protest from nature which may lead to its downfall. In this sense, we may say that every culture—since it is necessarily lived, developed, and transmitted by men—attunes itself to the vital requirements of human beings; as Malinowski shows, culture serves to satisfy irrepressible human needs and even conforms its standards to the more inescapable data of age and sex. But it does not stop there: just as it alters needs as well as satisfying them, according to what Gardner Murphy calls canalization, it also modifies as much as it respects biological dispositions corresponding to age and sex. We must be careful not to forget the extreme plasticity of man's nature. We do not therefore deny the idea of a human nature. It asserts itself clearly enough by offering resistance and clamoring loudly for its needs when it is thwarted by events; but we refuse to define nature simply as nature, and we have said that there exists a possibility for freedom. Because nature has this character of plasticity, it is in a certain way consubstantial with freedom, but it also can adapt itself to the influence of a culture—to the point where it is just as difficult to discern what arises from nature and what from culture as, in another connection, it is to say what comes from nature and what from freedom.[4]

Perhaps we should go even further than Mikel Dufrenne and say that here a demarcation between culture and nature would be not only difficult but impossible, and undesirable besides.

For the real individual, for each one of us in this world which is ours in language and experience, the sexed body becomes an element of personal destiny only to the extent and in the mode in which it is accepted and assumed. In accepting his body and its characteristics as the very heart of the personal history which molded them and created him, every man taking cognizance of himself takes a stand with regard to others, looks at others and knows that others look at him. Body and temperament are integral parts of a situation. When I accept my sexed body as an element of a situation that governs my existence, I make myself a member of a definite group, the group of men or the group of women—groups often highly organized, separated, even opposed in many primitive cultures, groups that are too large, fluid, even impossible to describe in the churning and rapid evolution of urban cultures. These groups are omnipresent, but they display so great a number of contradictory characteristics as to discourage attempts at an analysis.

But vague or precise, masculine or feminine societies are not the only groups to which acceptance of my body compels me to

[4] Mikel Dufrenne, *La Personnalité de base* (Paris: P.U.F., 1953), pp. 224–25.

give allegiance: in every field of society I enter, I accept myself only as a representative of many others who are like me. I am both the member of a group and its representative; and to the extent that I decide that I am a member whether I like it or not, I am clothed with one of the traditional images of the group I have decided to join. I am white, of male sex, one who either accepts or rejects a Christian or a secular tradition, or his roothold in an agrarian culture or in the drift to city or suburb. In many spheres, and not only with regard to masculinity or femininity, the outline of the original model has become blurred and sometimes tends to disappear in the all-too-rapid flux of global changes. Self-acceptance is thus acceptance of myself-for-others. The person is not only an autonomous center, an irreplaceable source of meaning and hence unlike any other; he is as well (even according to the etymology that assigns him a mask and a role on the stage) a myself-for-others.[5]

Yet the autonomous center and myself-for-others are one and the same. Interior source, awareness, dynamic project, and exterior appearance completely interchange their roles. One mind is not constituted in relation to another mind and for the latter, or one body in relation to another body and for it, but man in relation to other men and for them. It is this fact of being constituted in a relationship to others that reveals the person to us and to the others, in the same moving continuum of language and without the duality of meaning which the word *person* assumes for the analyst who kills when he dissects.

Yet a lack of analysis holds just the same danger as a lack of reflection. The whole ego can be flattened out into the triviality of a shallow myself-for-others; one of these secondary roles on the

[5] "On one hand the 'person' is the *subject of law*, the term and principle of juridical relations, an element of a community; in this sense, our word is directly derived from the Latin *persona* which in Roman law signifies precisely 'representative in *res judica*.' On the other hand, 'person' defines a subject, no longer the term or principle of relationship, but as himself constituting that relationship. The person then becomes an individual *charged with a role*, called to a function in the representative ensemble, 'a walk-on,' 'a personage,'—this is so true that our word has also taken on the meaning of the Greek word that translates it—*prosôpon*—at the same time that it again assumes the probably original meaning of the Latin *persona*." G. Fessard, *Pax Nostra* (Paris: Grasset, 1936), p. 44.

world stage can completely replace the personality, the entire ego can cease to exist and become merely a social and superficial self: an actress can acccept herself only as an adored doll, a student can think of himself only as a muscled athlete.

As a person I have a place in the group, and each human being ends in accepting his sex in somewhat the way an actor agrees to play a certain type of role: man or woman, this is to be a fundamental characteristic of my role in the human comedy on the stage of the world. This acceptance and its modes imply a style of life, a way of speaking, walking, and behaving. Such style and manners are suggested from earliest childhood, and each lives his sex in relation to the other, plays his given role—or refuses this role; then people speak of maladjustment, failure to integrate in society.

Issuing from a fundamental and universal relationship of personality, the acceptance of sex as masculine or feminine is none the less of the same type as the acceptance of all the other components of one's personality. It is neither a separable element nor necessarily more determinative.

SEXUALITY AND EDUCATION

The attainment of corporeality is the culmination of a genesis, and this genesis is in turn contained within a culture. It is impossible to discover or even distinguish precisely what in this genesis is determined by the physical datum and what comes from education, from the culture and its traditional images. Everything has been given a meaning, and the determining factors themselves are often cultural; the sexual datum is apprehended only at the end of an evolution which has given it a meaning. As Maurice Duverger writes, "from birth women are plunged into a system that tends to make them believe in their femininity."[6] Simone de Beauvoir analyzes at length some of the conditioning imposed on babies from the moment they are born.[7]

[6] M. Duverger, *La participation des femmes à la vie politique* (Paris: UNESCO, 1953), p. 132.
[7] *The Second Sex*, Book II, chap. 1, "Childhood." Margaret Mead's description of the very first education of an Arapesh, a Mundugumor, or a Tchambuli baby (the manner and time of carrying it, giving it the breast, making its cradle, etc.) is equally characteristic.

It is easy to stress the predominant role of education. The pattern of woman's passivity and man's aggressivity is cunningly imposed by a thousand and one attitudes and unconscious modes of behavior. Quite often the most unconscious insinuations are the most effective. Later, these modulations become more apparent. The little boy of seven or eight is asked: "What are you going to be when you grow up?" This is a question and implies action on the world. Before a little girl of the same age or younger, people will exclaim: "How pretty she is!" This is a statement and has to do with a manner of being. Perhaps in our day we will hear a statement which no one would have dreamed of making in the last century: "It is good for a girl to learn a trade so as to be able to earn her living!" Not that women worked less in the last century, but small provision was made for their vocational training in other than those very limited sectors considered proper for them. Quite possibly a concession such as the above will be linked to a severe condemnation of the evils of an era which overthrows the "natural order" (here confused with habit), and a trade or profession will be considered a last resort in case of involuntary celibacy. The evolution here is significant. But what will happen when, in a manner just as "natural"—i.e., accepted by custom—people ask a young girl: "And you, what will you do when you grow up?" It is no longer unusual, especially among the middle class in our new suburbs, that the same, unsegregated education is proposed for boys and girls.

But we haven't really reached this point.

From the very first day of his existence the child is enlisted, coaxed, cajoled, and forced to behave in a manner befitting his sex, without anyone taking the pains to know whether he is geared to this behavior either temperamentally or socially. The boy learns that he must be 'a good sport,' aggressive, ready to defend himself with his fists; never cry; not hang onto his mother's skirts, use blasphemous language, prefer football to music, not admit he is tired, and 'to be a man like papa.' On her side the girl soon learns, despite any inaptitude of temperament either congenital or acquired, to show her anger in a different way from a boy's; she learns that certain forms of irritability and pouting will be tolerated, that she is permitted to cry whereas boys may not, that quiet games are better than noisy ones, that she must not exercise too violently, that a doll should be preferred to a football, that she must avoid a certain language, and on many other points conduct herself as 'a little lady.' The innumerable facets of social domination which we use to impose these procedures of classification on our youth are evidenced in an infinite number of details, often unnoticed. The little girl is taught to sit and walk properly, how to wear her clothes, not to cross her legs, and a thousand other minor lessons which enter into her personality and, in case of need, prove the classification to be justified.[8]

While we must recognize gradations here according to social environment, it is still true that an orientation is received from the very beginning, and a direction imposed upon the biological differences. Education plays a basic role in the child's awareness of the difference in sexual organs and their existential meaning; this difference is suggested much less by biological factors than is still too often supposed.

The pressure of traditional images tends to justify the male and the female image at a most tender age. Only a few days after a child's birth people have been heard to exclaim of her behavior, "How like a girl!" Such a statement may well be misleading; the exterior genital appearance can be frankly ambiguous. If so, care must be taken to avoid the trauma caused in correcting, as far as surgery can, an error of identification. Psychological conditioning as regards sex is definitely established between the ages of two or three at the latest. It depends exclusively on education; the determining sex is that of the birth record and is not genito-gonadic. After this age the psychological shock of a return to the genital sex might have pernicious effects for the rest of life, because so much has already been contributed to a certain way of entering into society, and so "natural" has this adaptation been considered.[9]

As Marcel Mauss wrote at the conclusion of his more general study, *Les Techniques du corps*: "We are faced everywhere with

[8] H. Bloch and A. Niederhoffer, *Les Bandes adolescents* (Paris: Payot, 1963), p. 107.
[9] Cf. J. Lafourcade, "La Détermination du sexe," *Cahiers Laënnec* (June 1962), p. 34.

physicopsychological composites of a series of acts. These acts are more or less habitual and more or less entrenched in the life of the individual and in social history."[10] It is totally useless to try to sort them out into cause and effect. Introduction into society thus assumes a basic value; while the traditions of that society are not altogether rigid, their weight is nonetheless tremendous. But this ordering of the child's universe and the little man's progress in a world where everything is in its place, where each gesture and action is already delimited, specified, and localized in the fabric of the tribe, are reassuring and humanizing. In this way my body comes to live in society.

"Cases of invention, of positing principles are rare. Cases of adaptation are a matter of individual psychology. But generally they are governed by education or at least by the circumstances of the common life, by contact." This statement is true also of sexual differentiation, with a much wider range of significance. "It is due to society that there is an intervention of consciousness. The intervention of society is not due to the unconscious." This is another way of saying that in the transition from the biological to the human, it is the human that gives meaning. This is true above all of being-man and being-woman.

AMBIGUOUS ROLE OF THE CORPOREAL DATUM

There is nonetheless a corporeal datum, and its role is not zero; its determinations are means and obstacles, limitations and possibilities. The role played by the corporeal datum can not be isolated, it never appears save in the ambivalent meaning already bestowed on it by its culture.

Certain examples offered by Buytendijk are significant in themselves, but also in the way they are handled in a prudent attempt to adapt them to the conclusions of existential analysis.

We speak of a *grown girl* on the appearance of certain obvious physical traits, and when she herself experiences her first menses. We speak of a *grown boy* when he is able to work and begins

[10] Marcel Mauss, *Sociologie et Anthropologie* (Paris: P.U.F., 1950), pp. 384–86.

his initiation in a man's trade or calling.[11] The girl knows that she
has arrived at the frontier of the adult world when she is herself
conscious of a certain number of biological changes. In earlier times
this marked her definitive entrance into the adult world, whereas
today adolescence is prolonged for her as well as for the boy. Puberty does not have the same social value in the case of the boy. But
where an initiation or religious ceremony takes place to celebrate
the boy's arrival at puberty and mark his passage from childhood
to adult status, the contrast between the sexes is sharpened by
ceremonial rites that make masculinity an honor and a privilege.
Most often, on the other hand, the appearance of a girl's menses
is considered by men a sort of illness, no doubt slight but hardly
an occasion for a ceremony.

Where, then, do we place the distinction between nature and
culture, and which is the basis of the other?

More common examples are also significant, for instance a
gesture on meeting such as shaking hands.[12]

What is the nature of the handshake between man and woman?
There are several possibilities. Certain women extend the 'paw'
firmly. Certain men stick out a flabby hand. Between these two,
there are all kinds of gradations. Nevertheless, one fact stands out
in general—the man has a big hand and the woman a small one,
and the big hand is the stronger. But that is not all. Not only is
the man's muscular strength greater, but his grip is different. No
doubt it is the man's strong hand that encloses the small hand of
the woman, but the man *moderates* his strength. The woman,
whose soft, fragile hand is grasped, notices and feels this modera-
tion: she knows that the other knows that she herself knows it.
Here, reciprocity is not simple but double. The encounter of the
two sexes thus offers a tacit agreement, a dialectical relationship.[13]

This is an excellent analysis. But we have omitted several lines
that foreshadow the surreptitious intervention of cultural data,
in no way derived from the dynamics of the body: "The man experiences his corporeal existence as a resolute grasp on the world.

[11] Buytendijk, *op. cit.*, p. 352.
[12] *Ibid.*, pp. 323 ff.
[13] *Ibid.*, pp. 323 ff.

. . ." What follows is not deduced from the simple description of a handshake; it is an exposition of a meaning already assigned to the shaking of hands (a gesture by no means universal) within a culture where each of the couple has already acquired an idea of what is masculine, what feminine. "The man feels that the hand held out to him is less decided, less grasping, he perceives a person who is more reserved, less expansive, less aggressive—above all *less committed*. The woman perceives that the man has this feeling, and he in turn perceives that she has perceived it."

This conclusion only shows the impossibility of distinguishing between nature and culture and between object and subject. Each, through shaking hands, perceives his own subjectivity as it is acquired through a culture; in this encounter each confirms the idea transmitted to him of himself and of the other. He justifies a classification that gives substance to pseudo concepts, but the "nature" he encounters is particular to his own culture.

Is the taste for adornment, today ascribed to woman, linked to corporeal dynamism? Or should we really "expect . . . this demonstrative quality to belong properly and directly to the expansive dynamism found among males in the animal world? We have seen that a mane, antlers, brilliant coloring denote the demonstrative entity among male animals; that among primitive people it is the man who wears the gaudy ornaments, that, despite their gravity of mien and dress, men today retain their inner exuberance."[14] There is indeed a need to justify the feminine taste for adornment which appears as a curious inversion! Men, otherwise, outwardly manifest a marked awareness of their superiority. Is the superiority of the male sex also based on "corporeal dynamism"? History, economic necessity, the give and take of the marketplace, have collaborated until the opposition between the sexes is played out as much on the mode of conflict and defiance as on the mode of a search for love.

[14] *Ibid.,* p. 352.

MODESTY, STYLE, AND CLOTHING

Van der Leeuw writes that "all anthropology is in the costume," or, put differently: man is an animal who wears clothing, which is only a variation of the classic adage that "man is a social animal." Acceptance of the body is acceptance of a role to be played in the world and of a mode of appearing. Clothing is part of the style of life. Even if it is no more than a string or a loincloth, it is determined by a society, the insignia of the social group to which one belongs. Men and woman also have their insignia in a world where each assumes the garb of his role, the garb of the group or subgroup to which he belongs more or less of his free accord, or the garb of those he will join when he is free to make a choice. Again, society determines the moment for nudity, complete nakedness being often reserved for sacrifice and the approach of God—before whom no one plays a role. On the other hand, ornaments are increased when one plays a role for God, but before a crowd. Or, in secular society, nudity is linked to communion with domesticated nature and suggests nothing more than vacation time. Modesty directly affects this relation to another; fundamental, it is social and variable in its essence. Clothing, the insignia of our social role, is likewise the sign of our dignity, but this is understood in highly varying ways, depending on the culture. Modesty is "natural" in proportion as the particular society is "natural."

Modesty in a society begins when love is possible, and love is possible when man attains to a reciprocal knowledge and recognition which will place the sexes in opposition, of course, but will also permit lovers to invent at times a history that can eliminate this opposition. Born of love, modesty asserts itself with the growth of love, it becomes subtler and freer in proportion to the increase in opportunities afforded the lovers in social life and according to the type of this social life. Modesty is neither shame of the body nor shame at the physical aspects of love. "A pure heart is not ashamed of love; but it is ashamed if its love is incomplete; it upbraids itself if there is some hostile power which hinders love's culmination."[15] Modesty has no immediate connection with nudity, it is a confused fear of the possible use of eroticism for individualistic ends. Eroticism can hide beneath the mask of love, and the same gestures—instead of expressing love and the quest for interdependence, or a way of transcending the fundamental solitude resulting from cleavage with nature and one's own ego—are merely appearances and have to do only with the body. Modesty is a defense against the erotic approaches of the other. A prostitute who refuses to undress or have someone touch her before receiving her fee is not modest but defending her financial interests. A streetwalker who simpers and affects a thousand and one hesitating gestures and glances before taking off her clothes is not modest but clever and coquettish: she is playing her own erotic role in response to the erotic advances of the other. On the other hand, two persons with their bodies muffled up against the icy blasts of winter can exchange glances that carry the most erotic of invitations, and can receive an equivocal response compounded of connivance, promise, and acceptance.

Modesty can justly be called defense of the body, but it is a defense against what is lacking in love; it is self-defense against an erotic invitation which has not yet revealed itself as the language of love, or which has already asserted itself as a pure expression of desire; it is self-defense against an erotic approach which seems offensive in the very measure that it places the other outside the true dialogue, takes the other as partner in a game and not as the indispensable developer of one's own ego.

Faced with such obstacles, such barriers, such social deceptions, modesty organizes a timid game, awkward as truth itself. This game consists of questions and replies, erotic but veiled, loving but questioning, conveyed in a chiaroscuro of symbolic speech within our language, until finally all eroticism has become the sure language of love; then modesty, which is the result of love, blossoms forth as it discovers in this love its own deep meaning.

In societies where strict segregation of the sexes and clear distinction of social functions is the rule, modesty takes the form of

---

[15] G. W. F. Hegel, *Early Theological Writings*, T. M. Knox, trans. (Chicago: University of Chicago Press, 1948), p. 306.

tabus and stereotyped attitudes; it will assert itself more surely and freely when verbal communication between men and women is easier and more common. As soon as sexuality finds a peaceful mode of expression, love asserts itself more strongly as a personalizing factor; but here erotocism also finds it easier to play its role, and finds subtle excitement in advancing under a mask in a more sophisticated deployment of selfish desire. Its gestures are all the more apt to be understood as signs of interpersonality, to be taken for more than they really signify. The invitation to love can then be played out on two levels, and the erotic advance takes advantage of this ambivalence. But it is also the reason why modesty is refined when greater social communication between the sexes is permitted, and when more attention is paid to the meaning of gestures and their human significance than to the gestures themselves.

Fashion and clothing are elements of this dialogue; they also are weapons and arguments used in the battle of the sexes. They can be made to serve in an erotic enterprise as well as for defensive purposes. The range of possibilities in such symbolic language goes parallel with freedom of verbal communication and the interchange of social functions between men and women. But the role of fashion and clothing is not confined within the bounds of a particular and limited dialogue; this role emerges and enlarges at the same time as the language. Style and clothing are a social and human mode of being.

Fashions in clothing either accentuate or blur social differences according to the image of masculinity or femininity that they bring onto the stage of the world—from the workman in blue jeans to the beplumed music-hall dancer who becomes the doll of the adult male and his erotic games.

Style and adornment are linked to the mode of appearing in public. To adorn oneself is to present oneself to the other in a certain social role, and adornment has the function of showing the dignity entrusted to this role. A dancer's jewels may be artificial, but not those of the queen. Such adornment is not feminine, it can be worn by anyone who must appear in public and wishes to attach a value to his social role. Kings and princes of the Church adorn themselves as do women of the world, and more than many a young and pretty actress. At least until the seventeenth century, it seems that adornment and taste for elegant clohing were found more often among men than women. Not that this is in continuity with the greater splendor of males in the animal world, but probably because men had to "show themselves" in public as much as women and even more. That adornment became feminine after the French Revolution is largely due to the fact that the man of quality had become the bourgeois, one who works, and his wife, as guardian of the household, found herself entrusted with the role of appearing in society.

Adorned or not, my body is not a thing, it is a condition; dialogue with the outer world and with others takes place in words and gestures, and it is primarily through my corporeal condition and my sex that I am in the world with others—a world where each one knows that he will encounter others and is human only by this confrontation. The encounter comes first; and through it, man emerges and comes to know himself. Corporeal dynamism permits us to abstract one element of this encounter, but it does not allow us to characterize what is masculine and what feminine in any definitive and universal way that would have positive meaning for every individual, always and everywhere.

FUNDAMENTAL CONSTANTS?

Despite all this, can we define constant bodily data that are sufficiently basic to color and shade all sexual behavior? Can we find any physical conditioning that will determine a certain direction of the sexual differentiation? And what methods should we use?

To extrapolate from biology to the human being is to start out at the wrong end. On the other hand, any discussion of biological factors based on a phenomenology similar to that of J. J. Buytendijk is in danger of falling into the trap of the culture that engenders it—of universalizing, in fact "naturalizing," the Western phases of society at a stage where it had hardly begun to cast off its ties to agrarian civilization. The method by which Margaret Mead, in her book *Male and Female,* attempts an approach similar to our own is more likely to lead to a valid disclosure on this fundamental point.[16] In order to reach the core of the conditioning common to every culture, and different according to sex, she compares sexual determinations and their geneses in seven primitive tribes widely divergent in their categorization of male and female, their sexual values, and consequently in their ways of educating children. The mores of the Tchambuli, the Mundugumor, and the Arapesh, to which we have referred in an earlier chapter, are sufficient proof of the extremes in the area of her investigation. Now, by referring to such extreme cases it becomes possible for us to reevaluate our own behavior and to look for some conditioning that is universal. It then appears that there remain at least two constant data of corporeal dynamism, data susceptible of varying interpretations and cultural evaluations, but differentiated according to sex.

Sexual behavior of the little girl provoked by divers erotic stimulations or incentives tends to show a response of the whole body; this response is a corporeal attitude. The boy seems more inclined, in more or less symbolic form, to adopt an attitude of exaggerated emphasis on the phallus. The girl's anxieties and pride are focused on her behavior as a whole, while the boy is more concerned with his virility. There is no doubt that in such behavior the part played by culture is tremendous and inseparable from corporeal dynamism, but we are approaching the point where culture and "body mechanics," or techniques, are meeting.

A second element appears more clearly as a bodily datum; it relates to pregnancy, acceptance of which is difficult and special for the little girl. There is in this acceptance an element of "corporeal dynamism," not a development of the so-called maternal instinct which the young girl shares with the tigress and she-mon-

---

[16] *Male and Female, A Study of the Sexes in a Changing World* (A Mentor Book, The New American Library, 1955). Published for the first time in 1945, this book analyzes the relation between men and women in seven South Sea societies—Samoa, Manus, Arapesh, Mundugumor, Tchambuli, Iatmul, and Bali; in this light it seeks to examine the reciprocal relations of the sexes during the rapid social changes taking place in contemporary America.

key.[17] If motherhood is a feeling and a human function, and so has its greatness,[18] pregnancy is an important phenomenon in the biological order which the little girl must accept in her personal and social life. This acceptance is laden with artificial difficulties of a cultural order in our Western society where pregnancy, far from being treated simply as a normal event in a woman's life, is hidden and dissimulated both by habit and by social conventions. Here is a specific instance of a more general attitude among us, which has barely been breached: man feels honor-bound to deny his body, and multiplies his defenses of clothing, social rites, tabus, vocabulary, and gestures. Awareness of the condition is thus made all the more brutal, its psychological integration all the more difficult. The necessary acceptance of pregnancy and its inconveniences is accompanied by an awareness of more general significance: the burden of sexuality will be heavier for the girl, because of its consequences in the progressive stages of childbearing.

From this conditioning, the constant pressure of cultural traditions easily leads to the passive behavior prescribed not by "nature" but by a history. Passivity must be ranked high among the values of "femininity." Thus the man-woman confrontation is linked to the specifically human struggle for reciprocal understanding and recognition; the history of man and woman is then written in terms of the mutual defiance of the sexes, divided into two vast classes of possessors and dispossessed. At this point the conditioning of woman to pregnancy easily becomes "gynecological intimidation," a weapon and an argument; the "values of maternity" can be exalted as the "spiritual point of honor" of this alienation. Still we find in history's thread a perpetual reminder that love and the human values of intimacy create the compensation necessary and the counterpart required for personal development, and that defiance is overcome by the mutual recognition of subjectivity.

But this development is not inevitable and history in this sense has scarcely begun, any more than has the history of the relations of the sexes, or the broader history of political relations among

[17] Besides, a young animal fixes on the first animated being he encounters, not on his mother instinctively recognized as such.
[18] Cf. the following chapter.

men or of man's struggle with nature. The discovery of conditioning factors that mark a direction in biology itself does not lessen the variety of the dialogue. We are confronted with the conditioning factors of this direction, and not with foundations and structures of a definite and fixed nature.

Woman as such does not exist. There is no eternal feminine. But while the duality of the sexes cannot be reduced to a natural phenomenon, neither does it arise solely from the history of civilization. Genuine anthropology elucidates "nature" only in a concrete society where culture humanizes itself, only to raise new dangers of "denaturing" man, and woman.

CHAPTER EIGHT

The Confrontation of Man and Woman
as Dialogue and History

To write on sexual anthropology is to take as subject a relationship. The risk lies in forgetting this fact and arriving at illusory definitions and individualized characteristics in order to project an ideal and abstract man and woman. This would be not only an attempt to objectify a universal element of human nature, but further to apply it specifically to two groups of human beings. Such objectifying leads to physical and psychological dualism and perpetuates the opposition between the sexes which is ascribed to nature. Is this not sexual racism? Still it is not enough to observe that man and woman are different, that their roles in society differ, and that sexual relations are based on the biological difference to conclude that (*therefore!*) they have a different mentality and form two social groups.

THE INTERPERSONAL RELATION

In being-man and being-woman one must look much less for duality than for the interpersonal relation that forbids simple individualistic comparison. To think that man and woman have different personalities because they spring from two different sources is a mistake. We cannot comprehend the nature of sex or understand the masculine being and the feminine being so long as we consider them as proximate realities, comparable to one another but different and independent—even if independence is

126

reduced to the individual roots proper to each sex, to physical bases which become psychological through bodily dynamics. Of course Buytendijk does not go to the extent of specifying two different characters, but he ends by distinguishing two different sources of character.

This difference and separation he considers as evident in what each sex achieves independently of the other, due to the other, in confrontation with the other, but of itself. After defining the sexes in their duality, he analyzes the diverse influences of this individual achievement on the partner and at the same time what the other requires of that partner. Reciprocal giving is too often discussed in this sense.

Nor is the problem solved by defining the human person in terms of simple self-fulfillment and according to the existential project, as do Husserl and Simone de Beauvoir. That would mean to suppress the sexual difference, or at least reduce it to the level of social contingencies, because of inability to account for it in a manner that is mentally satisfying. We must agree with Simone de Beauvoir in rejecting objectivism and in refusing to reduce the person to a thing, by considering him as the result of a complex but scientifically knowable process. Still, it is not necessary to agree with her that the person is reduced to a pure possibility, defined only by the achievement of subjectivity, a point of departure without a goal. Nor can we agree that love is only a play of impenetrable mirrors, or a momentary forgetting of solitude in the mists of tenderness.

Conceptualization is impossible. Masculine and feminine, being-man and being-woman, are pseudo concepts. We must try to understand the nature of human sexuality, starting with the concrete experience of the encounter and confrontation of man and woman—not, we must repeat, of two individuals who come together, but an encounter in which persons recognize themselves as persons. But the more one tries to perceive the meaning of this experience, to understand or think about it, the less does sexual character lend itself to conceptualization as masculine being on one side and feminine being on the other. This does not mean that we intend to lose ourselves in vagueness, nebulosity, or cheap lyricism. The danger is serious, but it arises from individualistic specifications on this score, and many are its victims. Since rational exploration is difficult and has as yet scarcely begun, many are satisfied with naïve systemizations or seek the answer in dubious fantasies, echoes of sociological reports of the day, simple and uncritical classifications of ideas inherited from agrarian civilization. The worst of all is sentimental chatter, all the more harmful because, after all, we are talking about ourselves. Many marriages are mercenary, of course, others simple sentimental encounters, others still erotic contracts, but the man-woman relation is fundamental, and to understand it is to understand oneself.

The difficulty arises first of all from a question of method: a genesis must be studied as such. But there is also a question of object: sexuality is not a reality or, more exactly, the object of sexual anthropology is not a dual reality, of two existent individuals whom we must place in relation; our object is the reciprocity itself in which persons are individualized, the reciprocity of one being for another, otherness as a constitutive of the person.

Simone de Beauvoir is right in saying that woman becomes a woman under the gaze of a man, but one must assert with equal emphasis that man does not become truly man save under the gaze of a woman; the sexual differentiation is a phenomenon of reciprocal humanization, the appraisal of an existential difference under the gaze of the other, who addresses himself fundamentally to the bodily reality through which I situate myself in the human world. Here especially the curious and basic connection between being and knowing is revealed. To know the other is to become oneself; to be fully oneself is to know that one is for another. Man and woman become what they are only in the reciprocity of a bodily encounter which commits the one and the other, the one to the other; moreover, they test what they are only in this reciprocity. One is oneself only through the other; this is fundamentally expressed by sexuality.

Yet we must not limit our attention to the sexual union. In every encounter of man and woman, the same interplay of being and knowing has its humanizing effects, whether this be acceptance or rejection of the other. In every encounter the bodily reality, in so far as it is the being-who-has-become, the stage actually acquired in a genesis, is already presupposed; and by this bodily reality, whatever the nature of the encounter, each person manifests himself to the other as question or answer. In every encounter of man and woman, being-for-the-other is the first of all facts. But the encounter can take place on the subhuman level, and the human himself can evaporate in trivialities, the subject be dissolved in an anonymous "us."

The reciprocity of being-for-another is achieved through perfection of being-with, lived in the mode of intimacy. And sexuality is revealed in this dimension as a universal structure of the human being in genesis. Its development discloses what it is in principle: transsubjectivity, the real and concrete basis of all interdependence. Thus sexuality is at the source to the degree that each can only be given to himself as responsible for the other, each is himself only through the other. The mode of being one for the other is given before all experience, it is presupposed in acceptance as much as in rejection. The person transcends himself fundamentally, and this is revealed by sexual differentiation.

The opposition of masculine and feminine is the translation, the manifestation within a culture, of a fundamental relationship. The encounter comes first, the encounter and confrontation of man and woman discloses at the same moment their being-for-the-other and their alterity, an otherness that reveals itself down to the determinisms of the bodily data.

Thus we see appear the primordial decree which comes neither from man nor woman but which transcends them both, and gives them their concrete status as man or woman, together with an understanding of the character of personal engagement that affects their relationships. If the relationship of the sexes implies a responsibility of one for the other, it does so not only by an afterthought in the moral order, but because of a structural and primordial datum. Hence it is impossible to place a neutral undifferentiated human being above the masculine being and the feminine being, and to raise that human being to the rank of supreme principle. This being one for the other which defines man and woman is, from the anthropological point of view, a reality that cannot be reduced. It does not need to be transcended by a personal structure which might be superimposed on it: it is in itself a personal confrontation and, as such, is the primordial mode of the human being himself."[1]

Human sexuality is a dynamic interpretation, an expression appearing in various cultures, of a fundamental mode of being one for another. This expression allows us to judge the degree to which nature has been humanized in a given culture; it develops in a history where intersubjectivity, once it has appeared, can assume varying aspects. To base the man-woman relationship once and for all on immutable "natures" is one of the craftiest and most baneful ways of denying that there is a human history. Only culture allots complementary roles to male and female, roles that can only partially be reduced to a master-slave relationship even under the most crushing tyranny.

No doubt, as Henri Lefebvre says, "we have yet to see the disappearance of masculinity and femininity as rival entities living in defiance of each other," but the fluidity of roles has actually appeared in this conflict itself. What remains is the hope that mutual understanding may now also appear, as an opening beyond the class struggle and the present conflict, another form of dialogue.

In the division of duties, trades, professions, or points of view, there are always different fashions for one and the other of living life's conditions concretely, but it is also normal that the interlocking structure of the masculine and the feminine in the being-in-the-world shall develop and change with the conditions of life. Development and modification will be more evident whenever society changes more basically. Therefore, the modification of woman's role in industrial society which sociologists observe today is a perfectly normal phenomenon. The acceleration of history not only makes these changes more evident but also more pressing.

It is desirable to move toward equal status for man and woman, but not to an identification of the two sexes in the masculine way of life with its greater capability of autonomy in present-day social

[1] Erwin Metzcke, "Anthropologie der Geschlechter. Philosophische Bemerkungen zum Stand der Diskussion," *Theologische Rundschau*, No. 3, 22 (1954), pp. 211–41. This author is one of the rare theologians who considers human sexuality outside the usual perspectives of biological naturalism; his views are the basis of our reflections in this chapter.

structures. There is no question of ending in "insipid equivalence";[2] on the contrary, the point is to remove from the truly human differentiation the outward indications of woman's status of inferiority. Again, the point is not to suppress the differences but to make them more fluid; to speak of active differentiation instead of differences, of a relationship that differentiates. Besides, we must consider that this problematic equality will pass beyond present-day challenges and conflicting claims, so that the differentiation may appear in all sharpness, as a different development in the history of human unity, in that relationship which constitutes that unity.

There is no final subjection of one sex to the other. It is not true that woman is for man before she is for God. We either should put an end to all ambivalence, or say frankly that woman is a "defective male" or "halfway between ape and man." The relationship of man to woman is perhaps the only area where one may hope for realistic progress from the master-slave conflict to reciprocal responsibility, a true relationship between man and man. The hierarchy established by family and social groups is in any case mobile and does not affect sex positively or permanently, independent of codes and laws. On this precise point of woman's subjection we must agree with Simone de Beauvoir: this subjection is purely a historical creation within a given culture.

Woman, in order to maintain this confrontation and to remain a call and a response to the other, must guard her feminine originality, which she must seek both in culture and in the nature of her body. But corporeality is a shifting balance of the spirit-flesh unity of which woman is aware only under the gaze of the man. Woman's originality is no less great because it appears complementary, reflective, mobile. On the other hand, man's egotism, displayed in certain cultures to the point where only the male can claim true personal autonomy, is a way of being less a man—to such a point that the status of woman is a criterion of civilization.

What are often called woman's vocations or, as Gertrud von le

[2] Michel Deguy, *Esprit* (November 1960), p. 1687. "Do we not show the greatest possible contempt for woman when we urge her to conform to the mold of man, offer her the insipid equivalent of equality?"

Fort puts it, the three fundamental forms of womanhood, are three modes of confrontation, three modes of being-in-the-world: the virgin, the wife, the mother. Even virginity must be a manner to live with one another, if it is not to become infantilism or a pointless continence, or a form of repression.

The encounter is primary, the encounter not of two neutral and disembodied consciousnesses, or of two temperaments, nor of two bodies or of two minds, but the human encounter of man and woman which occurs in a history and a culture, and which creates in turn the history and the culture necessary for its occurence.

NEITHER COMPLEMENTARITY NOR POLARITY

It is not possible to speak of the sexes complementing each other or being in diametrical opposition.

On the lowest level, complementarity would mean a supplement added to something incomplete, that woman gives man something which he lacks, and vice versa. Or again, this word denotes the harmony created by the encounter of two separate elements. In neither meaning is the notion of complementarity sufficient to convey mutual responsibility, and still less fundamental otherness, the interpersonal and personalizing encounter. To speak of complementarity is to say that each individual has his own value before the encounter, that each posits himself as existent, with his own qualities sexually determined, and that the relationship which emerges afterward completes each of the subjects in uniting him to the other. In the first sense, of something incomplete to be perfected, each finds the part of himself that is missing, so that the end result, the final unity, is for each of them an androgyny rather than interrelation. That old myth evokes primitive times, before the separation; the Androgyne was the original principle before it was the reestablishment of the principle—a meaning which primitive intersubjectivity demythologizes and yet reinforces. In the second meaning, if we are thinking of the conjugation of two beings whose effective dynamism is redoubled by the harmony of their human encounter, the sexual relationship remains secondary and loses its specific quality: man and woman commune in things other than themselves, for a common good. This relation is similar to many others where again an attempt to be specific is made by declaring that what is imparted is something lacking in each of the two. The alternative to complementarity remains either pursuit of the Androgyne, the only complete being, or a relation among others, a means of obtaining together a common good.

Now, sexuality can be considered the sign of finiteness, in a more original and basic manner. If the relationship of the two is primary, neither is of value vis-à-vis the other; on the level of personal being each is only "for the other" and is defined by transsubjectivity. Each is the act of surrendering to the other in order to be defined by the other, and their intimacy is a relationship unlike any other.

It is not enough to speak of polarity and to distinguish two individuals oriented one to the other. To the meaning conveyed by complementarity, the word polarity adds the idea of a mutual tendency to the harmonization of individuals. This mutual orientation determines the relations of the sexes within a limited number of structures, schematizes the body and the spirit in separating their very conjuction, and determines this conjunction of man and woman. The relationship itself is no longer the history. Rather, the individuals evolve within a relationship forever the same. Here again a masked naturalism would have us believe that the body determines the spirit which itself determines the relationships.

The movement of love is warped in its sweep and drive if what we seek in the beloved are only our own aims, or if we strive solely for our own completion. Before the other we will at last have our identity revealed to us, under the form and charm of the beloved "Thou." My elusive destiny is manifest in palpable flesh and my soul in the eyes that look on me. I can lose myself in another and find myself; but what I obtain is both the void of which I am composed and oblivion to it—enchanting quicksand, indeed, proposed up by J. P. Sartre.

THE DIALOGUE

Our point is not the search for my ego or for the other half of myself, nor even the surrender or loss of myself. These are forms of human love, of course, but there are others simpler and more profound. It is not even a question of exchanging all one is in order to receive oneself from the other. Love receives nothing, exchanges nothing, makes no reckoning. What St. Paul said of love is true for all lovers: "Love bears all things, believes all things, hopes all things, endures all things."[3]

Love is born in the encounter, so that to love is already to be loved. But can I not love without being loved? Of course, but only in this world of today, with others, in a world where it is impossible for me not to receive some echo of love. To know that one loves without being loved is a worse agony than not loving, or dreaming of love. Not to love presupposes unconsciousness; to love without being loved is to become concretely aware that one is nothing without the other, and that one yet must go on living without the other.

Freedom itself is thus influenced by fundamental otherness; in this sense, the man-woman relation is primarily a dialogue—a dialogue that can result in communion and flowering in interpersonal unity, but that also presupposes a confrontation. There is no simple mutual adaptation, but a slow process of questions and replies. "This relation is fundamentally manifested as a history and as a dialectical process which develops by 'Yes' and 'No,' by 'For' and 'Against,' which can be neither anticipated nor assured, and which acquires substantive reality as one walks the unpredictable road of life."[4] The dialogue begins with life itself; early childhood is the prism by which animal sexuality is deflected and passes into language, so that it can never again be understood except through this transfiguration. This first dialogue is itself the culmination of a long human history. It continues and is echoed beyond the masculine and feminine genesis of humankind, becomes the encounter of languages, the history of the interpretations and harmonizations of the symbolic tongues of childhood. It also has its stages and degrees in the life of societies. It is both complicated and clarified at the thousand crossroads of social life, in the interplay of encounters necessitated by collective life. It refines itself slowly through the long hours of shared life.

This dialogue is the atmosphere, the element, in which love be-

[3] I Cor. 13:6–7.
[4] Erwin Metzcke in *Lumière et Vie*, No. 43 (July–August 1959), p. 50.

tween two beings can spring up and ripen. Starting with sexuality, it can lead to the personal intimacy of *I* and *Thou* in a mutual acceptance of responsibility for the other. This dialogue can become intimacy; it is always extremely delicate; deviations and misunderstandings are always possible. We see here, in the form of dialogue, the transition alluded to above, from the Thou and I to "being with"—a genesis in which the relationship is primary and the person is defined as such in a dimension especially stressed in phenomenology. But if the person is the relationship and if this relationship defines man and woman as two sexual beings, it is a fundamental dynamism, it is transsubjective, something to be achieved and therefore subject to rejection and failure.

Indeed, we here encounter the Bible teaching so often played down because it comes to us from a different culture: "God created man in his own image . . . male and female he created them." Theologians, unfortunately, speak to us too rarely of sexuality as an image of God, image of the Triune God whose Persons are defined solely in their relationship to one another.

Hence it will never be possible to describe the sexual difference. Any objective description of what is masculine and what is feminine is forbidden to us, but we know the reason. This differentiation is a history which we must construct each day in a dialogue that differentiates us and makes us other in making us ourselves. We no longer have fine didactic categories for defining male and female, but we understand better the personal foundation of sexuality.

Sexual anthropology leads us to a social dimension at the very heart of our freedom. Here also, and here fundamentally, man is the social animal. Beyond the various manifestations of sexuality, the deep reciprocal responsibility embodied in a shared life reveals itself. There can be no self-satisfaction, there is only a dialogue, a *praxis*, which is also, at its various levels, the conflict of love.

This dialogue engages us from the first moment of the human being whose concrete genesis it is; but its wide resonances and subtle chords are heard only within a complex collective life, at the end of a long history. In spite of millenniums of humanity, this dialogue has only just begun; as man's dialogue with nature through technical activity is as yet only in the first stages of transforming the world. Sexuality, like all nature, first manifested itself as ritual. There is no automatic encounter of persons; this encounter was invented, and it invented man. But, as we have said, the exchange of woman was first an economic matter. *Commercium* preceded *connubium*, as Marcel Mauss has emphasized.

The interpersonal encounter makes use of sexuality in the quest for intimacy. Only on this level may we find, not indeed an answer, but an indication of the direction of the quest; every person learning to love knows that he is himself only with the other. Thus I can know why I am not simply a human being, but a man or a woman, a call and response to the other sex.

The man-woman dialectic is fundamental, a foundation and not a product of history; on this point we radically disagree with Simone de Beauvoir.

But in the historical development of this dialectic, in its realization throughout history, man and woman appear face to face and recognize one another. This recognition is always unpredictable and can never be categorized, but can simply be noted sociologically in one concrete society or the other. Sexuality does not lead us to invent love, love reveals to us the meaning of sexuality. Man and woman do not create an interpersonal reality; but if the person becomes the relation and being-for-another, that person reveals me to myself as masculine or feminine in the encounter where I recognize myself as a person because I am being recognized.

MOTHERHOOD: VOCATION OR "GYNECOLOGICAL INTIMIDATION"?

The usual rebuttal offered to those who, for whatever reason, consider femininity a pseudo concept, is made in the name of "woman's vocation to motherhood." Woman was made to be a mother, it is inherent in her being; education prolongs her role well beyond the conception and birth of her little one—this is written in her heart. Thus a strictly feminine role is revealed, a role that is determined by physiology and psychology.

Many objectors find it difficult to imagine that one can mistrust the alleged determinations suggested by morphology, such as the reification of characteristics, without downgrading the role of motherhood. Many of them see the rejection of their sexual individualism for the sake of intersubjectivity as a road to insipid neutrality. We should repeat, therefore, that to consider sexuality as a fundamental relationship is not only to consider the individualistic conception of sexuality a partial deviation, but also to reject sexual neutrality as an empty abstraction, forever indeterminable. Intersubjectivity establishes love and determines the subjects. Differentiations are in no way lessened thereby, but become fluid and can be explained only by a reciprocal genesis.

Thus A. M. Henry, for example, found no other way to answer Simone de Beauvoir than by referring to a "woman's nature" that reaches its perfection in maternity.

> The supporters of a certain feminism, the most extreme of all, think there is no female psychology, or at least that what is called female psychology is only the heritage of certain customs or certain social behavior, which a different behavior can change completely. This view underestimates the deep roots in woman's being and nature—including, and even primarily, her psychology—of the goal allotted to her, which is motherhood. Whether her motherhood be real and physical, or adopted, or spiritual, it is in some way the pole toward which woman's . . . mode of being, of thinking, of looking at the world, of judging, is inclined.[5]

According to this view, there is a "woman's nature," and also a "female psychology." The basic argument is that maternity is "woman's goal," a purpose that defines her as woman and leaves its mark both on her body and her character.

But this horizon ascribed to woman's destiny may seem too narrow. The excessive limitation of her social role leads to revolt. Adrienne Sahuqué wrote as early as 1932: "Motherhood: here is the fundamental fault from which arise all physical, moral, intellectual, and social disabilities. By their tendentious writings, how many doctors every day make themselves the apostles of this gynecological intimidation!"[6]

---

[5] A. M. Henry, "Théologie de la féminité," *Lumière et Vie*, No. 43 (July–August 1959), p. 117.
[6] Adrienne Sahuqué, *Les dogmes sexuels* (Paris: Alcan, 1932), p. 256.

Would fatherhood then become a man's goal, characterizing him even in his highest social functions, as Louis de Bonald imagines? Fatherhood and motherhood would then be two highly diversified vocations of two individuals reconcilable only in the marriage bed, destinies with effects and repercussions on various levels of social life, without ever exchanging their roles. We should then no longer speak of the human species, but of a human genus divided into two animal species. Then let us have the courage to say, with St. Thomas as well as with Proudhon, that one of the two species is defective.

To tell the truth, the very purpose of man's relation to woman should make us ask what is the principle, and the final purpose, of that relation. But in the study of a genesis the principle is revealed first. Now, acccording to the able analysis of Gabriel Madinier, the man and the woman are principles in the unity of the family. "Any other unity is made up of beings already formed, while here we have a unity which is original. The family is the highest unity, because it is not a resultant unity but a unity-principle."[7] The unity of the couple is the principle of being, the couple makes the unity exist as subject.

But we must at once stress the fact that the parents give life to a subject, that they bring a person into the world; they are the principles of a being who will enter into their love as a third party, a being who will become *Thou* for each of them.

The unity of the couple is a principle only in a history. The purpose of education is to create, to practice, to develop freedom. The child raised by wolves would not be a free subject, but wolf. And if education is the genesis of liberty, it is also the dialogue and the history by which the child slowly becomes *Thou* for his parents. Through them he is placed in global history and in the adult collective world. There are substitutes if the family fails to effect this introduction, but they are only substitutes—adoption, the state. Where conjugal intimacy has ceased, another substitute is to entrust the child to one or the other of the separated parents. But in the optimum situation which is the goal of our inquiry, the

[7] Gabriel Madinier, *Nature et mystère de la famille* (Paris: Castermann, 1961), p. 60.

child depends directly on intimacy and the unity it implies: he needs the disinterested love of his parents for each other simply to be loved for his own sake. While his presence involves certain dangers to which we shall refer, it can still reinforce the unity that is his own source, that of the "family we." The principle and the destiny of the child, of the man and the woman, is the very self-giving generosity of love.

History divides the couple's indivisible parenthood into paternity and maternity. There was first of all a global parenthood; then, as it created its own history, this parenthood divided itself into father-hood and motherhood; but before it became specific, it designated the parents' joint role.

While these observations are commonplace, they support our analysis. It is the "union that differentiates," according to a formula dear to Teilhard de Chardin; but the union comes first. Far from being rooted in individual difference (physical or psychological)— the foundation of motherhood is neither the womb nor the instinct for her young that woman shares with a tigress—truly human moth-erhood is rooted in the development and the history of the man-woman relation. It will flourish all the more in the differentiation of the maternal and paternal roles in proportion to the intimacy of the union. Motherhood is not an individual vocation, but a social role. As such it becomes a component of personality, a consequence of the fundamental man-woman dialogue.

CHAPTER NINE

The Human Sexual Being and the Choices of Love

Continuity and discontinuity: these two terms define human sexuality as against animal sexuality. There is continuity in the genital activity, in erotic impulses, life exploding in the species and the species recovering individuals through the dissolution of their bodies after death—the external bond between love and death in the fatality of cycles; irradiation throughout the psychic structure of an energy colored with the waters of the same springs whose echoes reverberate on the various levels of the body and the mind. There is discontinuity because the mind controls the power that permits it to encircle the earth but did not do so. Genital activity and activity of the mind, the erotic search and the spiritual search are correlated and independent at the same time.

Opposition is possible also, as we noted earlier, between sexual activity and the transformation of nature through work. The indirect relation to nature through practice is not in continuity, but discontinuous with the immediate relation through sexuality.

Conflicts are not unavoidable, but man must find an equilibrium for his sexual behavior in the face of a series of obstacles.

Opposition between genital activity and the psychic structure. Unrestrained genital activity exhausts and kills the psyche; a balance is necessary simply to safeguard the autonomy of one's actions, a counterbalance based on the difference between animal and man in the bond that joins individual and species. If we can speak of regulation on the level of the animal species, this concerns the species only; the individual does not exist as such, he is for the species. Man, on the other hand, is a person, his genital activity is individualized. On this personal plane he must try freely and consciously to find an equilibrium which has not been granted him in his struggle for existence. This balance must be reached so that the person may continue to fulfill himself as a person.

Opposition of two modes of relating to nature. The humanization of nature and man's naturalization through work, or his socialization, oppose the unbridled satisfaction of his sexual instinct. The balance, imposed here by social pressures, may again be placed in jeopardy. Society curbs the sexual instinct and allows it to erupt only in certain limited circumstances—formerly in religious festivals, the bacchanal for example, or in puberty rites; today in secular holidays and often in individual celebrations (we celebrate, but we can't do it every day!). On the other hand, brutalizing work sends man back to sex and instinct as a simple way of rejoining nature in its immediacy. We must condemn here not the artificiality of the modern world, but that dehumanizing work which sends man back to nature himself dehumanized.

Opposition in the human dimension of alterity. The other desired as a person, is in opposition to the other, desired as sexual partner to satisfy a need. To take a woman as the object of desire is actually to destroy her as personal partner; in extreme cases it leads to sadism, her pure and simple destruction. If she accepts this reduction as her destiny, she becomes a masochist and tries to recover her personality in narcissism. In this perspective with all its possible degrees, Helene Deutsch's observations remain perfectly valid.

Contradictions arise from the desire or will to carry one of the dimensions of sexuality to its limits; they are the result of an abstract idea and a bias. A single way remains open: to abandon the maximum in one dimension in order to find the optimum that will be balance and synthesis.

Man's specifically biological sexual organization has no built-in controls; it neither plans nor prepares any kind of solution. It simply tends to destroy itself in carrying an animal tendency to its limit. On the other hand, activity that is properly human, cognitive, and loving, tends to direct sexuality to the point from which it will mediate into all areas of behavior, including the most intellectual. Man must discover and set for himself an optimum in sexual, genital, and mental activity—this is human freedom facing the contradictions of sexuality. Whereas animal sexuality is regulated by the cycles of species and the Darwinian struggle for survival (a victory of the species over the individual where genitality in the end imposes on itself a sort of self-regulation though basically this regulation may not necessarily stem from sexuality), human sexuality can unfold only in a loving dialectic. Sexuality derives meaning from man, man understanding the biological dimension, not the biological dimension insofar as it determines man.

But the transition from animal sexuality to the loving dialectic is already effected when man is man. Love is not the result of a choice; love conditions the choices among the ambiguities of sexuality and societal life. We are not free to love, and yet is not the one we love the elect of the heart? Who is the master? How can this irrepressible dynamism be controlled?

If sexuality in itself is prior to the logos, love is a language, and Eros supplies it with its signs and symbols. Like language, love arises and develops with humanity, it is a dimension of man's genesis which like all else is relational. Endowed with language or capable of love, man no more chooses to love than he chooses to speak. He appears before the other, and from then on he is in a situation where not to love is already to have rejected love; that is, unless the individual remains at a prehuman stage, a-logical, unable both to speak and to love. For such a man, who has emerged into a language and a human world, sexuality is the audible echo of a totality which swells and expands beyond its own frontiers in search of meaning. As the totality that seeks to find itself in love, mankind becomes the undefined network of intersubjectivity which is embodied and particularized in the flesh of the couple. Love both invents itself and calls out to us, never completely fulfilled but always as complete as the world itself—to the degree that love is authentic, to the degree that we find ourselves only in losing ourselves. Others dream of losing themselves without undertaking this voyage. However, one does not choose to love; love begins when there is no longer any choice; one can only choose not to love, either from fear or from selfishness.

Our refusal may be made for the sake of money, for political reasons, to affirm one's selfhood, or for ascetic reasons and loss of self. We can refuse for the sake of God. But apart from all human aspects, what is God other than man's inner search for a spiritual source, the Source of sources, or the search for an empty tomb, too quickly christened the dark night of the soul—or, deeper still, the dreams of a troubled conscience, reminders of God's absence?[1]

If our selfishness is more or less conscious, "woman" evokes only the idea of a comfortable retreat and the "family nest." This is sheer fibbery: priests and nuns, and even more the champions of various ideologies, deceive themselves with a thousand fabricated hardships of a difficult day-to-day existence. With our sacrifices for an ideal or for the future we cleverly conceal from ourselves our fear of throwing ourselves into the sea of a great passion in which man is metamorphosed. All this is not meant as an invitation to eroticism, but to take concrete relationships seriously.

How, then, justify chastity? There is is no point here in enumerating and criticizing its social justifications, but we may ask how chastity can be legitimately introduced as one of the modes of living in search of optimum and specifically human sexuality. In this light, chastity would seem to be the renunciation of eroticism as the privileged expression of love, but not the renunciation of all modes of intimacy. The difficulty then is to find a true expression of love in everyday activities. This difficulty is not theoretical but is inherent in the life that takes the greatest risks. There are many ways of expressing love, but they all commit us to losing ourselves in order to find ourselves, without knowing whether or not we shall.

---

[1] Simone Weil wrote something to this effect: of two men who have had no experience of God, the one who denies Him has more chance of coming close to the truth. But this experience itself can only be a form of union, it can only spring from love. Love of what? So-called experiences of God are often delusions; they can only be delusions if we cast man aside. Isn't this the meaning of the discourse which Matthew records from the lips of Christ, the Judge of all at the end of time: The saved and the lost both ask, "When did we see You poor, starving, naked?" We must stress the verb as much as the adjectives. When have you *seen* Christ? The answer is plain: only when you have seen men, when you have loved them, not with a universal, anonymous, aseptic love, but with the efficacious love that binds concrete relations and works to change conditions (Matt. 25:31–46).

The task of the person vowed to chastity must be to find a human way of expressing love in a more universal but still concrete language.[2]

To be saintly is to kiss the leper out of love. It is heroic to kiss him out of a sense of duty, but that may also stem from a strange masochistic yearning, so that each of the two is less a man after the encounter. The leper might rebel at being the object that allows the bountiful Pharisee to feel that he is rising to a peak of humaneness, a caricature of love.

We do not choose to love, we surrender before love, we cast ourselves into the stream without knowing what wave will come to bear us up— Yet every day we must invent fresh gestures of abandonment, gestures in which we risk ourselves completely.

But such abandonment presupposes choices and breaches.

In its free decision, sexuality appears both as a promise because of its irradiation throughout the whole psychic structure, and as a threat because of its tendency to go to the limit. It appears as a promise because the desire for personal communion and a preference for the other as a human is inscribed in the whole body; as a threat because in its completely carnal aspect sexuality strives for maximum satisfaction, to the detriment of the person.

THE LOGIC OF POSSIBLE CHOICES

We must choose because we must love; sexuality has no true rule, it recognizes only free control. Joined to intersubjectivity, our choices may be viewed either as they affect the partner, or with regard to the autonomy of the choice.

Regarding the partner, as sexuality reveals the depth of transsubjectivity on the human level, there are two possibilities:

[2] Not that these few remarks on chastity suffice either to justify or to explain a celibacy accepted for religious motives. We would have to place ourselves in a more global dimension of human development, go back to one of man's origins including and surpassing the sexual dimension, and discern authentic modes and possible deviations in the motivations of religious dynamism. It is sufficient here to stress that to be chaste still means to love and to love passionately, and that chastity does not exclude all modes of intimacy; rather it seeks modes beyond eroticism. Thus any study of chastity should include a study of friendship.

1. A *choice for myself at the cost of sacrificing the other*, without whom I am nothing.

2. A *choice for myself at the cost of sacrificing myself*, since without the other I am nothing.

Sexuality can blossom only in the second attitude. I am unable to fulfill myself, to balance my own sexuality, except by my total surrender to the other. What exists is not an isolated man and an isolated woman, each seeking self-fulfillment, but the coming of the two face to face. Sex has no individual foundation even on the biological plane. What exists is the person, who is not a neuter but a relation; what exists is the man for the woman who is man only through her, or the woman for the man who is woman only through him. What exists is this encounter in a society where animal sexualism can reappear only in opposition to this personal relationship.

Regarding the autonomy of the subject, which assures his own control over the course of his life and tends to his own personalization, the choice bears directly on history; it is understood in terms of time.

The choice is therefore:

1. To humanize the movement toward animality and surrender to *undefined moments*.

2. To define one's own history, to synthesize the gestures of love in a controlled future development, which is to opt for the *continuity of presence*.

In the first choice, preference is given to the paroxysmal moment of the sexual act; in the second, preference goes to the history of which this act is only a privileged expression.

Again, this logical apprehension is confronted with a fairly broad range of human choices made in one or the other of these two perspectives.

There is still a third possibility. Since one does not choose to love, owing to an ultimate confusion between love and sexuality, one can dismiss sexuality from the field of action of a free man, which is to say, *not choose*.

A choice in regard to sexual life is said to be impossible because sex is stronger than any human will, and behavior in this domain springs from a sort of fatality; or else sexual behavior is judged according to standards which have nothing to do with specifically human sexuality. In both cases, sexuality is considered to be in opposition to history, either because, as fate, it has ascendency over social life, or, on the other hand, because social life and history have nothing to do with sexuality.

THE CHOICES

1. *Not to choose.*

We can decide not to choose, or we can declare it impossible to choose, for diametrically opposite reasons:

Because we wish to make full and perfect use of all—even contradictory—aspects of sexuality; this choice leads to a consideration of the most revealing myths concerning love, such as that of Tristan and Isolde.

Because, on the contrary, we are afraid of a passion that in itself tends to the maximum, without concern for contradictions; this refusal eliminates love at the same time as the myth. Puritanism offers typical examples of elimination of this sort.

TRISTAN AND ISOLDE

Here the myth is the symbol of an impossible accord, the triumph of passion in death. The complete and mutual surrender of two freedoms is identified without shade or reservation with bodily union; two freedoms become but one. There is no distinction between sensual pleasure and freedom.

An opposition remains, but it comes from society. A union is total only if it is restricted to the couple. Otherness is found only in a society, but in this case it is manifested in the mode of division. "The admirable episode of the exchange of swords makes this clear. When the king comes upon the lovers lying asleep in the cave, he substitutes his own sword for his rival's. The meaning of this is that in place of the obstruction which the lovers have wanted and deliberately set up he puts the sign of his social prerogative, a legal and objective obstruction. Tristan accepts the challenge. . . ."[3]

If the lovers cannot be alone in the world, at least their presence in the world will have no other purpose than passion. Everything should be put to the service of this passion; but others refuse. Never has the universal placed itself entirely and unreservedly at the service of the particular, even if the universal itself dissolves, phenomenally, into conflicts between particular interests. If not hostile, society will be indifferent.

The reason, an even deeper reason, is that the will to place oneself beyond all opposition is a way of stepping away from history and its ties. The absolute of the unity sought would be elimination of time for the lovers or the perpetuation of the paroxysmal moment. But in the last analysis the attainment of complete unity, the merging of all contradictory lines into one, together with the assurance of endless duration, is granted only in the tomb.

Their love involves no decision; the intervention of the fatal philter, which they have taken by mistake, is an illustration of the inevitable necessity of a passion that sweeps aside every resistance and all willing. Yet their will to place themselves beyond all choice is very deep. Thus the communion of the two lovers appears, not as the realization of a free act, but as the fulfillment of a destiny, the unfolding of a fatality.

The theme of fate and death are linked in this love which rejects both the undefined moments and the continuity of presence—which wants them both: the moment that lasts forever and the oneness of two persons, apart from the rest of the world. But only death will give the lovers this definitive bond.

Down to modern days, various versions of this or similar myths, such as those of Romeo and Juliet, or Orpheus and Eurydice, have told again of this desire to reach the maximum in all spheres and at the same time to concentrate all eternity into one moment.

[3] Denis de Rougemont, *Love in the Western World*, Montgomery Belgion, trans. (New York: Pantheon, 1956), p. 36.

PURITANISM

The absence of a choice, or the refusal to consider sexuality as a criterion of choice, prevails also in the family which has no myths, this time simply because it has no love. The puritanical family is the best example of refusal to choose for fear of reaching for the maximum which all passion implies.

If the myth of Tristan and Isolde carries us beyond choices and oppositions, the puritanical family leads us to a nether plane. The myth deals with the situation of lovers who set themselves apart and reject the world or history; the puritan wants a place in the world and the elimination of all sexual aspects revealed in love. There is no myth here, for the hypothesis is that sex has nothing to do with being-in-the-world.

The choice is made on other grounds. Rules for the union of man and woman are external to love as well as to all other expressions of sexuality. Marriage is an association of interests. These interests can be highly diverse: if they are economic and familial, marriage is a consolidation of capital; if political and national, the royal or diplomatic marriage is considered an alliance. Religion is brought in to reinforce sexual prohibitions: husband and wife should found their union on other things than "the works of the flesh," which are obscene; the foundation of an indissoluble union should be the vow that is taken, civic duty, family tradition. Even in the best of cases, it still remains necessary to offer family, legal, and religious alibis for the weakness of the flesh.

Here a complete separation is reached between sexuality and the encounter of man and woman. Adolescents will of course be allowed to dream of love, pardonable in very young people, but to found a family is something more serious! Family stability is based on interest, and such stability is still further assured if this interest is money—and God, who has made marriage indissoluble, is invoked in support of money.

Thus the encounter of man and woman is based either on economics or on politics, or again on religious alibis advanced for fear of real commitment to a passion. In order not to run the risks of loving passionately, we love no one and justify ourselves by "spiritual points of honor." A certain misogny, a contemptuous way of speaking of woman, along with a life of irreproachable morality—an attitude also found among priests—is often no more than a way of justifying ourselves for not loving truly or concretely.

While lovers step aside from sordid social realities—economic, as when the king marries the shepherdess, the princess the chimney-sweep; or sociopolitical, as Romeo and Juliet—love is banned as sordid by respectable economic and political society. But sexuality is total and cannot be banished, it will reappear to avenge itself and surge up again in its animal as well as human dimensions. Love can spring up even if it is forbidden, but it will then be a rebellion against social barriers and even against society itself (romantic love). The carnal instinct will also reassert itself, and in the puritanical family adultery becomes acceptable if social appearances are safeguarded. The woman treated as an object will take her revenge by becoming a "mistress"; we will not go into the painful entanglements of repressed love: the mother-son, father-daughter fixations, or all the other intrigues that delight the world of the popular stage.

Here emotional feeling is taken only as a sign of weakness, and the smile of contempt that is feigned for the sexual act contributes to the attitude which considers physical love a banality.

2. *The choice for self at the expense of the other.*

To choose means already to have accepted sexuality and certain of its limitations.

DON JUAN

This time the myth does not concern a couple but an individual. His aim is to seek the complete development of human sexuality insofar as it is human, but in himself and for himself. Here to be loved means that the reciprocity of love is prized as an added fillip to love of self. What is sought is the development of sexual drives along the lines of one's own personalization; the other is taken into account solely insofar as she conditions the growth of one's own personality.

Many degrees are possible, but the tendency expressed in the myth of Don Juan is clear: the criterion of success in uniting with an individual is the degree of satisfaction obtained by the momentary act, the deployment of a certain psychic aura being a component of success. Psychic means and freedoms are made to serve the complete success of an act which is an end in itself. Finally, this development takes place along lines that we have described in our chapter on eroticism. The choice is made, a firm choice both for one's self and for the undefined duration of moments.

Sometimes the unifying purpose of such a life is seen in the search for the Absolute, but this explanation is superficial. Only in literature can Don Juan persist in his quest for an ideal love, for a pure vision of woman, without being engulfed in encounters where the only thing affirmed is his own ego, and that only for a moment.

The myth's finale is not necessarily the commander's banquet, or the lament of a family or a society rejected at its very roots, nor is it the dead-end of eroticism; the result can also be the Girolame of Milosz's *Miguel Mañara*. Girolame reveals true love to Don Juan, but this love has become impossible, or requires a complete conversion, a kind of inner renewal.

The social image of "woman" has prevented the invention of female counterparts of Don Juan—so difficult does it seem to concede to woman the will power that is the necessary mark of a man of the type of Don Juan! The will power that might reinforce her revolt is more readily converted into a will for enslavement. The slave takes her cunning and overwhelming revenge on the master. Or else we attribute to woman "masculine" qualities and cite Messalina, George Sand, even Catherine of Russia as examples. The type can also be degraded in the "wayward girl" or the "maneater," or simply the nymphomaniac; this is then reinterpreted as a sign of weakness.

The same weakness can define a man's conduct, and it is even possible that this case is more frequent. "Don Juanism," writes

A. Hesnard, "is a falsely virile sexual mentality that conceals a lack of masculine sexual maturity."[4]

MYTHICAL AURA OF THE FILM STAR

Choice for one's self can be pushed to the extreme of eliminating all relations between man and woman. In the Brigitte Bardot or Marilyn Monroe myths, the other is not even present, for we are not dealing with an actress but with her image. We cannot meet an image, but we can at least enjoy it; there is nothing left but "these little pleasures." This myth does not concern a couple; it does not even concern a person, but a body, whose measurements are more important than the dialogue. In eliminating all personal encounter there is a tendency to separate love from instinct. In the myth of Don Juan, love is governed by instinct, there is no connection between love and instinct. The union of mind and heart remains a legitimate search, but no longer has anything to do with "physical love." The sexual act becomes commonplace and is not taken seriously because it has literally ceased to have meaning. Unfortunately, this is what some of our contemporaries call sexual liberation.

Films, strip-tease, and a large output of cheap books have vulgarized the search for sensual pleasure without personal encounter, and have introduced the masses to this degradation of physical love.[5]

Whether it is a matter of pleasure by proxy, as in the film image, or reduction of the sexual act to triviality, no contempt is shown the partner taken as object and there is no question of woman's enslavement; in purely physical encounters in the technique of love-making, mutual contempt is shown for an act which neither of the couple takes seriously, nor do they attach any importance to it in human terms; it is simple pleasure, fleeting and ambiguous. Pleasure is separated from friendship, which itself no

---

[4] A. Hesnard, *Manuel de sexologie* (Paris: Payot, 1951), p. 207.

[5] "These attitudes, and the absence of any personal encounter they presuppose, combine to produce the prevalent mental transposition of sensual pleasure." Cf. J. Evola, *Metaphysique du sexe* (Paris: Payot, 1959), p. 17.

longer has anything to do with sexuality. Sex is no more than an animal need which each satisfies according to his own taste.

But if in human experience sexuality is defined by the confrontation of man and woman, it will rise again and avenge itself—either in encounters that awaken the heart or in transferences and repressions. Or else love and sexuality will reveal their psychic dimensions under forms which are degraded in the same way as the sexual act—the cult of film stars by their fans, vague dreams and image-worship, or attachment to fleeting ideologies that call for grouping into "cells," or the organization of gangs and clubs. The search for communal association tries to find objective expression on another plane, where dissatisfaction nonetheless persists.

In such things energies are wasted and no attention whatever is paid to the satisfaction of sexual needs; loss of self and loss of time assume the false appearance of realism.

3. *Choice of the other to the point of sacrificing self.*

This choice means at least implicit recognition that in the confrontation of the sexes each person is constituted by his relation to the other. This is the relationship that develops into love. What are the components of love in the perspectives opened by this choice?

The free act and choice are placed on the level of human sexuality in the confrontation and transsubjectivity of the man-woman relationship. It is this relationship, where each recognizes that he is nothing without the other, that should be confirmed and promoted, and should strive to affirm itself in the reality that is the unity of the couple. This relation can be established only to the extent that in the free act the other is considered as a person and as the other; which means that the free act of each has as its object the very freedom of the other; each of the two, in the act constitutive of his own love, wishes for the other to make a free decision concerning that act. Here then is no alienation but a confirmation of the sexual relation, if indeed the other, and he alone, constitutes me as a sexed person.

Love succeeds only if this attitude is mutual. Each considers the freedom of the other, each has as his purpose the growth of the other, the subject of his love. Hence each makes himself completely vulnerable to the other and is nothing without the other. Love becomes the amorous dialectic that constitutes the free person.

This union, like the search for love that preceded it, is based on sexual drive and eroticism, in the sense that these are not only the condition but the necessary expression of love. Of course each of the partners should control the sexual impulse where it leads to a maximum negation of the freedom of the one he has chosen, but eroticism intervenes as the expression of this freedom for the encounter to reach optimum growth, in harmony with personal union and not in maximum negation of the person.

This choice is not on a lower level than passion; it is not a limitation placed upon the passionate will of the lovers to go beyond the point where any choice is possible; it is not a will of the type we find in the myth of Tristan and Isolde. If it were, passion would be preferable. It is, on the contrary, the only possible way to pass beyond the limitation placed upon their attitude by the linkage of love to fate. Without ceasing to be passion, love can make itself the history of destiny. A more personalizing way of loving roots the relationship in a mutual choice in which each considers the person of the other, and wants the other's freedom to unfold within and through a love in which each desires the ever-increasing growth of the other's life. Genuine love is a free but devouring passion and can grow even as it creates a history. It is not based on Eros and does not lead to momentary paroxysm, but puts eroticism, all eroticism, at its service. Eroticism is nothing more than a privileged mode of expression in a history which is the outgrowth of the reciprocal gift.

This love indeed creates a history and stands revealed in the history that it creates; it is a perpetual advancement of the other; what it seeks is continuity of presence in progressive reciprocity. The paroxysmal moment of bodily union is not the goal but the expression of love. The goal is the union it expresses. Also, it is not set apart from society; on the contrary, the other's development is willed, mutually, in all dimensions of the person. Love is itself the history of mutual personalization.

One can dream about this personalization, think of it only, and all the while lead a puritanical life. As an example we have the ordinary couple, or any of the many shades of moralism and accommodation. But in its fundamental meaning, what we are trying to describe is nothing other than the Christian ideal of marriage as typified by Christ's love for his Church. St. Paul explains: "Husbands, love your wives as Christ also loved the Church." Now Christ "emptied himself completely" and counted himself as nothing; he loved in sacrificing himself. Christ and the Church are not two complementary realities, and neither are man and woman. This is the profound meaning of St. Paul's teaching; it should not be minimized by overestimating marginal directives peculiar to one culture or one period of time.[6]

That this love arises from Christianity is not an article of faith, but it was born in Christianity, it is Christian or post-Christian. It simply presupposes a deep grasp of the significance of ideal love as it was pointed out for the first time in the New Testament. An illustration is given by Anne Philipe in her admirable book entitled *Le Temps d'un soupir:*

> Love is a source, a source reason; the world becomes fruitful; love is astonishment, the feeling that a miracle has happened, and at the same time something that we knew before, a return to the Lost Paradise, the reconciliation of body and idea, the discovery of our strength and our weakness, attachment to life and yet indifference to death, a certainty never revealed yet moving and fluid, something that must be won new each day.
>
> You were my most beautiful bond with life. Through you I came to know death. When death comes, I will not feel that I am rejoin-

[6] "New and Old Testament writers, wanting men to understand the meaning of God's love, naturally chose for their parables human love as it was experienced in their times and, basing themselves on these conditions, tried to find symbols for grace which they could set before the world.

" 'Husbands, love your wives, as Christ loved the Church,' says the Epistle to the Ephesians (5:25), not by dominating them, as would be your right, since you are their head, their chief, but 'as Christ delivered himself.' Here was the point of the parable. . . ." (Francine Dumas, "Situation de la femme: lois, moeurs, et images," in *Christianisme Sociale* [November–December 1962], p. 687). But all too often the accent has been placed on the husband as "head" of the wife to make an archetype of a contingent situation.

ing you, rather that I am following a familiar road already known to you.[7]

The ties to history are here brought out in a striking way.

This type of love leads to the optimum potential, and allows us also to underscore Eros' fulfillment, in opposition to the puritanism that moralizes to the point of immorality. Driven to sacrifice of self Eros becomes Agape. Eros and Agape are too often contrasted; but the contrast is entirely formal, and creates a false dualism. Love has its source in freedom and in Eros, it makes Eros its servant and expresses itself through him, to the point of sacrificing him for more freedom if necessary. Love leads Eros to the dimension where there are more opportunities for development of the other, before whom one is completely vulnerable. The lover's vulnerability can be expressed even more fully in transcending Eros through self-sacrifice—really counting oneself as nothing before the other as Christ before his Church, even though this symbolism, and the reality at its source, are almost forgotten in our day.

Hence the man-woman dialogue which we have extracted from the anthropology of sex concentrates on the interpersonal relation of a man and a woman, a union which tends to create a new human reality and which will write its own history within the frame of human history.

Such union is certainly neither easy nor usual, especially as in this perspective there is something worse than not to love, and that is to love without being loved. The growth of union is difficult, the dialogue is an uncertain groping. At times the promises of love are fulfilled only very slowly.

PSYCHOLOGY AND THE CHOICES OF LOVE

We, like many psychologists, must be satisfied with outlining a sort of typology of the states of consciousness of sexuality. What are the modes of awareness, the attitudes and behavior behind them, and what concept of sexual life do they assume?

[7] Anne Philipe, *Le Temps d'un soupir* (Paris: Julliard, 1963), pp. 49–50.

OBJECTIFYING ATTITUDES

Awareness can begin with a simple need, sexuality can be envisaged in the mode of relation to an object. Thus various attitudes are adopted for the purpose of satisfying this need.

The need may be experienced as proceeding from a compulsive dynamism even beyond the individual organism, a dynamism emanating from the very abyss from which the individual has sprung. It draws us to an attitude of cosmic communion, a search for the Lost Paradise, the animal Eden of the spirit, and to a yearning for radical oneness with nature. But man begins precisely with the fissure he wishes to fill in. This need can be satisfied in two different ways: orgiastic festivals, uninhibited eruption carried to the point of paroxysm, or the ritualistic inclusion of erotic gestures in an attitude which is fundamentally religious and pantheistic.

The need can be felt simply as organic and individual. The sexual act can be included in an ensemble of compulsive attitudes to balance an organic tension; it will have no other particular significance. When emphasis is placed on the pleasure derived from lowering tension, sexuality will appear as one of the possibilities in the search for pleasure.

Sexuality can also be reduced to its instrumental role, and sensual pleasure considered merely as incidental to the satisfaction of a specific necessity. In this attitude, the sexual act is considered merely as the natural means to reproduce the species, and conscience must then reduce the sexual drive to this instrumental role.

PERSONALIZING ATTITUDES

Here awareness begins on the level of effectivity, and sexuality appears as it affects the person in his subjectivity.

It can be experienced as affecting subjects individually; it becomes an effective mode of discovering, affirming, or losing one's identity in confrontation with the other. This attitude leads to conflicting love-play and at the same time to a complicated network of sado-masochism.

Sexuality can also be understood on the level of human love as the symbolic language of intersubjectivity. Here there can be no question of anything other than interpersonal relations, giving and exchanging, so that a community of subjects will come into being.

These basic attitudes condition many acceptances and rejections, furnish criteria of choice, and often become dogmatic in reinterpreting all other attitudes by relating them to some single interpretation of sexuality. We ourselves are reinterpreting, but without dogmatizing and with the least possible bias, when we select the optimum of personalization as our criterion.

In the case of objectifying attitudes, sexuality has no decisive meaning on the personal plane. No doubt many manifestations remain on the level of these analyses. It is harmful to over-emphasize their meaning and to overload conscience with diverse and unwholesome tabus. The question is whether sexuality's whole meaning is exhausted on these levels. If sexuality has no decisive significance on the personal plane, if it seems definitively marginal, the mind itself is threatened with degradation to the point where it is denied a place in a domain rightfully his.

The attitude of communion with the cosmos, no longer a faint echo of our origins but now grown systematic, does not allow a critical examination of its "ecstasy." There is no escape in a blind alley! In an industrial society, "communion with the cosmos" would be profaned in forgetfulness of work and end by merging into the facets of hedonism. Apart from sexuality, if we reject as entirely the simple equilibrating aspect of our bodily condition, do we not refuse ever to be in love? Finally, puritanism gives primacy to the function of reproduction, to the point where the child, and the social position it is to perpetuate, influence the sexual encounter and the marriage, minimizing the first and emptying the other of all sexuality. The child itself is a means, the person has his place outside all sexuality, in the world of objects. One can go still further and in the name of morality which is more lenient toward injustice, refuse to be drawn into the quicksands of Eros. The better to avoid passion, we often think of the absence of love as a virtue. But in all these attitudes we shall never come to know more than the slight ripples on the coast of a fathomless sea; without ever leaping into it, we may yet give the impression of a veritable drowning of the soul as we sink beneath the logos.

All these attitudes narrow the horizons of sexuality, because they make it into an object which is already an abstraction and a prejudice, preventing an understanding of its full meaning—that sexuality is a principle, and all-embracing.

Judged by its effect on the individual subject, sexuality is the foundation for each man's struggle for his own "ego" in confrontation with the other; it sanctions the fragile encounter but lets the battle of the sexes go on and on. Only at its summit, when sexuality expresses itself in interpersonal relationship, can it really be channeled into language and history. No one is a person except with and through others; love makes the person.

CHAPTER TEN

Toward Conjugal Intimacy

> "I swim by your side in the warm, clear water, I wait for you to appear in the doorway under the wisteria. You say 'Good morning' to me, and I know your dreams, your first thoughts on the fringes of sleep—and yet you are a mystery.
>
> "We talk: your voice, your thoughts, and the words you use to express them are the most familiar in the world to me. Each of us can end a sentence begun by the other. And you are—and we are—a mystery."
>
> ANNE PHILIPE, *Le Temps d'un soupir*
> (Paris: Julliard, 1963), pp. 48–49.

When the gestures of Eros become the ideograms of love, the magnitude of the interrelational network that establishes the man-woman dialogue from which we emerge is particularized anew, concentrated on the confrontation of one man and one woman, and it becomes a source of new life. It is the rebirth of a social life in its germinal state, a history beginning with the tenuousness of all dialogues; there is complete certainty of reciprocal giving, yet each day all must be invented afresh.

As a new relational reality which replaces two earlier individuals, a new autonomous center which makes "I" and "thou" into "we," the confrontation leads to communion in a new interpersonal subject. Love personalizes the two lovers; it makes them all the more personal by giving a concrete expression of the interpretation of its dual components: a unique subject unlike any other, entrusted with a role surpassing anything either of them could have, each of the two has become one with his role. There is no longer any distance between seeing and being-seen; the reciprocal relationship has become a "We."

THE HUMAN CHARACTERISTICS OF LOVE

We shall deal only with the relationship of the two lovers, not with the "we," and shall follow a purely phenomenological procedure in trying to discover how they can best develop human sexuality, without recourse to other criteri than sexuality itself.

The *foundation* of their love is their freedom: its principle is alterity. The close network of interactions, the polymorphic environment that existed before all language, when sexuality erupted in the exuberant expansion of species here becomes expressive, conscious, and salutary even in the zones of freedom it has not created. It becomes the reciprocity, particularized in the couple, of giving and mutual dependence. In the relation of these two lovers, everything that appears as the other simultaneously shows itself as a value of freedom; and the freedom of the one who gives is necessary for the other to be free. They love one another unreservedly, simply day by day. And each day their love is just as fragile as is their freedom, which can unfold in acts but can just as easily be submerged in them. Because love is rooted in the heart of freedom, in autonomy, each is nothing except by and for the other. The ultimate meaning of sexuality is here revealed as the principle of love, in a concrete transsubjectivity.

The *purpose* is the intimacy created by this reciprocity. The irreducible originality of this social bond comes from the fact that it is based on the very otherness of the two in love, and not on the participation of two complementary beings in a common good. Participation of two beings in the same good can take the place of love, but there is nothing original about it. The very originality of the man-woman relation becomes the purpose of love. Insofar as it is human, sexuality finds fulfillment in the reciprocity of two freedoms, each given to the other. To the degree that otherness is more clearly and concretely perceived day by day as the source of love, intersubjectivity grows into intimacy.

The *result* is a community that is unlike any other, because man and woman are freer and more united than in any other social tie. As the two personal monads particularize the basic relationship that makes them persons, a new form of unity begins. Like two haploid gametes in a single living cell, two free beings unite in the new being of their love, and here their history begins. But here also their differentiation is accentuated in proportion to their unity, because this unity does not exist primarily for the species, or primarily for the individual. More basic, it determines their very existence. It is this unity that differentiates.

The *condition* is that of the fusion of all free acts, all histories. Continuity of presence must prevail over the dispersal and dissolution in undefined moments. This dynamism must create its own history, and authentic intimacy must remain the personalizing element. It is a difficult achievement, for love, the constitutive activity of freedom, cannot establish itself as an object, exhaust itself in any act, or be solidified in any objectivation.

FRAGILITY OF THE "WE"

The "we" of the lovers oscillates between history and the moment, between freedom and fatality.

The spirit of giving unfolds and is generally expressed in bodily union, a convergence of the erotic drive for maximum fulfillment with the reciprocity of subjects who make it the expression of the best possible humanness. But there is still a conflict between eroticism, in which animal sexuality continues to seek fulfillment in the human being, and the freedom seeking human expression in eroticism. Erotic tension continues in the search for maximum satisfaction in the moment: but finding its fulfillment there, eroticism is in danger of devouring itself by destroying personalizing love. Moreover, the two lovers are always tempted to shut themselves up within their intimacy, to seek escape from difficult choices in a passion that will lead them to dream their love away in the mythical manner of Tristan and Isolde, instead of incorporating their love into collective history.

The lovers must cut themselves a path in the forest of social ties, but they may also get lost in it. If they fall to one temptation or the other, or take some other easy way out, fatality will take the place of freedom. The moment of bodily union becomes the symbol of the perfection to be achieved, and the vain desire to perpetuate that moment prevails over the history that must be made; the ties of love and death will entangle the lovers in a dialectic of mutual possession. The idea that love can be freed of all conditions imposed by society will prevail over love as it should be lived. By dint of dreaming of the future, love's actuality becomes a passing emotion in that its principle tends to fluctuate between freedom and eroticism.

Instead of remaining a fundamental social relationship, the man-woman dialogue thus is in danger of being lost in the erotic search.

The gift of the body should be the expression and not the culmination of love. It must not be the terminal point of the man-woman dialogue, but the beginning of intimacy, the foundation of a new history.

OPENNESS TO HISTORY: THE RISK OF THE CHILD

Lovers cannot escape all these risks without welcoming another: to have a child.

The solution must be found in sexuality itself. Any solution outside love would be a pointless invitation to renounce that love. If the bodily act, and all it presupposes of joy in mutual possession, is not to be an end but a beginning, not a momentary accomplishment but the expression of a love open to history, it must accept the risk of a child. This risk, inherent in sexuality, is certain to break the closed circle of endearments, and the charm of being only two. By accepting in advance the possibility of a child and his upbringing, the partners commit themselves to make a history.

If the gift of the body as an expression of love includes the risk of a child, it is impossible for the lovers to remain alone in the world, to reject history, to shut themselves off in their new being, the intimacy of their love. The mythical ending of a dual egoism, androgyny, fades like a shadow: the child breaks the circle of sexuality from within.

Through the child, the bodily act itself accepts the risk of casting love into the stream of history and society. The relationship becomes known, a public matter. Yet the lovers accept this vulnerability because their new being will become a new society in the eyes of men. Thus the surrender of the body cannot remain a simple expression of love like a private language for only two, it must also express that love before the eyes of all, before society. Because the risk of a child is accepted, love makes itself known and exposes itself to the judgment of men. The bond tends to become a social institution; the child compels the lovers to hand themselves over as a "we" to society. And as such, the child becomes a vow, even a challenge, to the extent that the lovers see him as one who will make their love a reality in the eyes of all.

But even the wanted child presents a risk. He compels the couple to deliver themselves into the hands of a history not of their own making, to unpredictable natural and social determinisms that they will have to organize and surmount together. It is of course possible for one or the other of the couple to prevent the child's existence; in this case of total opposition and refusal, the child's existence is dependent on their will. But in his positive existence, as in the matter of health, the child is also dependent on conditions that cannot be foreseen. Like their love, he is placed within the evolution of the solar system; in this sense, as they used to say, it depends on them or on the sun. More serious, a third and demanding matter is the danger that he may become the exclusive center of attention for one or the other to the detriment of their love.

THE MARRIAGE VOW

Acceptance of the risk of a child compels the couple to surrender their love to history and to society, but they want their acceptance to be based on their love, not only on the risk. The difficulty is compounded.

If the bodily act is not the aim of love, neither can it be merely a means of encounter in the maximum intensity of sensual pleasure. In any case the child cannot be considered either as a simple means to justify the bodily encounter, or as the exclusive aim of sensual pleasure.

The gift of the body must be reciprocal, total and irrevocable, at the very moment it is accomplished. As an aspect of erotic attraction, this act should be the unequivocal and total gift of two freedoms, so complete that each of the partners is willing to sacrifice himself if reciprocity is not assured. Each must commit himself to history; it is the fascination and the danger of love that the incipient history must also be founded on this love. What remains is that this gesture and this total gift be unequivocally joined before society.

There is only one solution: to make the gift of the body, including the risk of a child, the symbol of total and irrevocable surrender. Since eroticism, in developing its own specific aim, tends to make love a chase to possess, to have, the body and soul of the other, it must be transformed into an act through which each places himself freely at the other's service, in and for the pleasure itself. This presupposes perfect reciprocity, for any failure on this score leads to total sacrifice, or to masochism, or at least to withdrawal into more commonplace and less personal zones. Compensation is sought elsewhere, even if the rules are kept and conventions respected. It is always easier to look for pleasure outside marriage, and to keep up an honorable façade, than to give oneself to the other no matter what. But where true reciprocity exists, the mutual gift of the body can be made into a free and public and final decision to give oneself unreservedly to the other.

To become the social expression of a definitive love, the sexual encounter should be the fulfillment of a solemn vow taken before society, in history. Specifically it will be the vow taken at the time of marriage, which makes the search for sensual pleasure unequivocal and personal for both. This vow is the solemn expression of a love that will be manifested as the days pass by. The present is already lived as something that cannot be changed; love has risen to such heights that it seems inconceivable it could ever suffer change.

Such a marriage is *indissoluble* not in regard to sexual requirements, but because of the history it inaugurates. Those in love desire that the gift be made forever and without return. Love's fragility is fortified by the fact that it is expressed solemnly and publicly. The vow assures continuity of presence against dispersal in the moment. From the start, bodily union is made an expression of a perpetual giving.

Marriage is *monogamous*. It excludes all other persons from the same degree of intimacy; any other union is rejected which might debase the first union to a level of possession of property.

The act which constitutes both the fascination and the danger of love becomes its immediate mode of expression and at the same time the realization of the free and mutual gift. It consummates desire but begins history. As a free act, it casts off all temptations to look back. There is no longer any cleavage between enjoyment and the mutual surrender of free subjects.

The choice of continual presence, as against inconstancy, bestows a significant value on this moment; already the unity of bodily presence objectifies freedom in history and permits love to realize the exclusiveness and permanence to which it aspires. This intimacy will be broken only when the bodily presence is withdrawn—by death.

The solemn, public vow taken before society makes love a free decision. The partners assure each other that they are not merely pretending to give everything; they cut off in advance any possibility of turning back or of making another comparable gift. By exteriorizing and binding itself under the laws of an institution, conjugal love insures itself against its own weaknesses and manifests itself as a particular community in society.

SOCIAL ROLE OF THE FAMILY

Family structures cannot be transposed into social life even by analogy. Still less can society be conceived as a hierarchy of families, that hierarchy which conservatives of the last century, after Louis de Bonald, believed they could discover in feudal ties upon which they looked back nostalgically. Society is a mesh of far more diverse elements, an equilibrium of structures whose mobility has been accelerated. The dynamic tensions in this field of forces are the present result of the development of fundamental dialectics, and the master-slave dialectic is of as much importance in human relations as the man-woman dialectic which is connected with it. Hegel has shown how this dialectic of opposition and separation conditions man's knowledge and understanding of man, and that it is at the basis of human relations and of history. On the other hand, the man-woman dialectic is a dialectic of union, rooted in a relation to nature, and plays an intervening role in the master-slave dialectic. The two dialectics intermingle, and their effects on each other reverberate, as Father Gaston Fessard has frequently pointed out.[1]

Jean Lacroix has shown the devaluing of fatherhood. Transposed into social life, this bond justified a hierarchy, an inequality with condescending benevolence which finally deserved the pejorative term "paternalism." Little by little, these bonds become like those between equals and brothers.[2]

Many sociologists investigating the social functions of the family overlook the essentials. Indeed, the sociologist is always tempted to reduce the person to an assemblage of functions, and in the process the family vanishes together with the person.

Some of these functions are obvious—the economic function for example. If the family is no longer the large family of agrarian civilization and the unit of production, it is now in its more restricted form the unit of consumption. But this compression has caused it to lose its former fundamental role as a transmitter of inheritances, property, and traditions. The principal function of today's family appears to be education, whereas the increasing cleavage between generations, of knowledge as well as of experience, renders that function more and more feeble and uncertain after a child's first years. The speed-up of history has made the father the witness to a world already outdated, someone who can offer little guidance to his son. Conflicts of authority between the generations have become more and more sterile. We see fewer

[1] Cf. especially "Esquisse du mystère de la société et de l'Histoire," *De l'actualité historique*, Vol. I, pp. 121–22.

[2] Jean Lacroix, *Force et faiblesses de la famille* (Paris: Éditions du Seuil, 1949).

revolts of this sort, but they have taken other forms. Individual protests against the discipline and rules of the "cellular family," denunciations of the family as a closed circle or cell, lose their acuteness in a world where the torpor and warmth of the "family nest" is available only to those who have renounced any real activity in our present world.

To find the true function of the family in society, we must first recognize the new shape of the political dimension. Man is man only through opposition in a struggle in which he risks his life, and it is after this struggle that he is known and recognized as a man. The human being is born of this radical confrontation; he is not man in an extension of the biological element, but in breaking with it. We do not mean that the life of man has ceased its evolution, but that biological evolution is only one conditioning factor in the ever increasing and gigantic mutations of the mind. Biology can serve as guide neither for a plan nor for a norm of action.[3]

To understand the social function of the family we must follow the path we have traced earlier; we cannot start from a sexual need and proceed to the couple that constitutes a social mode of response to the requirements of altruism and procreation. We must begin on the higher level of the mind and its requirements. In other words, the function of the family tie is to be found in its meaning.

With all its conflicts, and through them, social life tends to unify. Among the types of unity it seeks to realize, Gabriel Madinier distinguishes three modes of association that mingle and intersect.

Cooperation produces concerted efforts toward a common end. The unity is partial; those who cooperate are concerned with only one aspect of life; while they strive together for the same end, they are not oriented toward one another, or only in an imperfect and secondary manner. The bond that unites them is some exterior, communal task.

Assimiliation expresses the genesis of a common will to live,

[3] Contrary to what some inattentive or hurried readers believe they have gathered from the works of Teilhard de Chardin.

such as the will that creates nations and makes peoples of different races and diverse traditions into "brothers." The differences can be resolved, without putting an end to discord and oppositions. We find examples among the new nations. All kinds of conflict remain possible—among families, professions, social groups, or classes; in interests, preferences, and enthusiasms.

The sociologist is fully at home with these two modes of association and the analysis of their components. In the same way, legal ties and social relations, and the ideas of man and woman they presuppose, are accessible to him in laws for the man-woman encounter and for marriage. The same cannot be said of *intimacy*.

> Human beings are no longer brought together by a common role, nor dissolved into a sort of collective soul or common mentality; but even while keeping their own identity, they exchange their inner riches and personalities, take pleasure in the one whose *presence* is entirely addressed to them, surrounding and upholding and enchanting them. This new mode of association must be analyzed all the more precisely because it is extremely delicate; for while the first two modes fit easily into our caterogies of aims and identities among human groups, *intimacy* transcends to a degree our logical ways of thought, which separate and juxtapose the elements.[4]

Apart from marriage, intimacy can also be realized in friendship, which the Greeks defined as "man's preference for what is human," and even in good fellowship. But love is the privileged example of intimacy, and the most one fruitful for society.

> Because intimacy leads to union, it is the realization of the most perfect type of social existence: human beings who give themselves to it (or at least strive to do so) lose nothing of themselves but find their fulfillment in establishing the "we." The purpose of this union is not some good work or outward arrangement; its source of being and its guarantee lie within itself. It is brought about for itself not something else, and far from drawing its meaning from a larger whole as a cog in a machine, intimacy gives a meaning to all the rest.[5]

[4] Gabriel Madinier, *Nature et Mystère de la famille* (Paris: Casterman, 1961), p. 95.
[5] *Ibid.*, p. 97.

Perhaps more stress should be laid on the emergence of the person in its relational essence. Can those who love lose anything of what they are when they discover that they exist through and for another? They themselves are this exchange, carried to its furthest limits[6] and particularized in the bodily encounter from which a history must be constructed. Each defines and differentiates himself further as he gives the other his due place—the whole place, simply. There is no inner sanctum, no inviolable center of mystery; inwardness becomes what it should be: one's self under the other's gaze; it consists in this perfectible relationship.

Thus the family is the place where the most fundamental social ties are revealed, and it is the normal place of a man's apprenticeship in social life.[7] Love is characterized by the fact that the presence of the beloved has become as indispensable as the air I breathe, the other is necessary to me as such, sacred, he gives life charm and zest; life no longer has meaning without him. Even death does not destroy this bond. The lover can say truthfully like Jordan to Maria in *For Whom the Bell Tolls*, "Thou wilt go now, rabbit. But I go with thee. As long as there is one of us there is both of us. Do you understand? What I do now I do alone. I could not do it with thee. . . . Do you not see how it is? Whichever one there is, is both." Merleau-Ponty comments on the profound association revealed in this kind of love: "We die alone, but we live with other people; we are the image they have of us; where they are, we are too. Once again and to the very end Jordan submits to that movement which binds him to others and to things, and which is beyond judgment because it is the condition of all happiness and all unhappiness."[8]

The union can be broken only by infidelity—not really broken,

[6] Lévi-Strauss, as we know, has shown that the human being is revealed only on the threefold level of exchange: exchange of goods in the form of potlatch, which calls for a gift in return; exchange of women, having particular roles within the clan as in its outside relations; finally, exchange of experience through language.

[7] Jean Lacroix, "Phénomenologie de l'aveu," *Recherche de la famille* (Paris: Éditions Familiales de France, 1949), pp. 199–212.

[8] M. Merleau-Ponty, "Man, the Hero," in *Sense and Nonsense*, Hubert L. and Patricia Allen Dreyfus, trans. (Evanston, Ill.: Northwestern University Press, 1964), p. 186.

but it will become clear that there is no reciprocity, merely the illusion of love.

There is no such thing as fusion. Androgynous unity—if such could be an aspiration of sexuality—is not the vow love makes. Love desires a union in which the lovers are present to each other in what is particular and unique to each. The individuality of each becomes a source of happiness to the other, for their union is based on this individuality. It is what makes them mysterious to each other, mysterious as the source of life itself.

The absolutely indispensable social role of the family is thus the very liberality of love, since it reveals and particularizes both the fundamental otherness and the first social bond.

OBJECTIONS

But this paradoxical bond between a sexual drive seeking mutual appropriation, and the intersubjectivity that makes it the concrete expression of being-one-for-another—it surely is a dream that can never come true? Can we spend our entire lives trying to carry out the decision of a moment? Has not love aimed too high? Of course, the decision does not go beyond the demands of sex life, of making a success of it. But isn't this too much of an ideal? The best is the enemy of the good; can lovers realize such a continuum in history? No doubt, as Gabriel Madinier writes, the couple, "makes us feel, in *my* love for *thee* and *thine* for *me*, that I am not an individual, but rather the terminus of a relationship," but it is never more than the "precarious and approximate realization of a community of fruitful intimacy."[9]

We are familiar also with arguments in the past regarding the purposes of marriage and their order of importance. So many philosophers and moralists usually name procreation as the first purpose of marriage. Have we done them justice in speaking of the child as a risk?

Two questions we must meet. One is from the sociologist who asks if we have given sufficient attention to custom in elaborating such a "theory" of love. The other is from the moralist who wants

[9] Madinier, *op. cit.*, p. 57.

to know whether our concept of married love, as a unifying history and creator of the family community, would not be more convincing if this love were directed toward the child?

We have considered conjugal love in its perfect form. But it is an experience shot through with weakness, instability, and flux, in which periods of boredom follow after passionate and violent desire. We must take this instability into account.

But first we must answer the moralist who questions the ideal itself and asks if we are giving adequate foundations to family life.[10]

THE TWO ENDS OF MARRIAGE

Moralists call procreation the primary end of marriage, intimacy its secondary end. Although their terminology has its place, it cannot be transposed unchanged to anthropology, where we limit ourselves to describing the genesis of a reality, choosing the line whereby its essence is best revealed. It is obvious that two normal human beings, even if they desire children, marry first of all because they are in love. We have said nothing more. But this is not what the moralists have in mind. They want to emphasize that the child is not a means. Similarly, speaking of intimacy as a secondary end, they affirm that neither is the conjugal "we" a means. We have said so too. The elaboration of these two propositions will show the divergencies and differences in emphasis among those who examine the question.

Do we not reduce the importance of the child when we make him a condition of true love, especially when we acknowledge him as a risk? Why not rather speak, with Gabriel Marcel, of the "creative vow"? Here one can immediately oppose the other alternative: to make of love, especially ideal love, a condition of true fecundity. But does this not minimize the fundamental relationship which love particularizes?

The child is not a risk in the sense that he becomes an obstacle to secret meetings and fleeting pleasures; intimacy has nothing to do with these hidden zones. He is a risk to the true intimacy of

[10] The next chapter answers the sociologist.

the couple. He is a risk because he is not the result of willing and acting, is not a result at all. He cannot be considered exclusively as the consequence of desire and love, nor simply willed as the result of bodily union. He is not just the result of an act performed to produce this result. We may not again separate husband and wife from the mutualness that constitutes their love, again give value to them individually and consider their union only a task undertaken for a common good. We must not see them as the meeting of two wills for mutual pleasure, and to undertake a common task of education. Once we do so, we can no longer consider their love in its authenticity. To speak of the child as a risk is to say that he is neither a purpose nor a result; that his dependence on the will of the parents is only relative and partial. He is a subject, unpredictable as such, and already has his absolute value as a person. And he interferes with their intimacy as a subject, not as a possession.

Because of his possible presence as a subject, the child is the supreme risk that threatens the couple's largesse. Present at the very heart of the liberal love of his parents, he is at the same time the realization and expression of this liberality, even when his existence is not certain, but only possible, expected, and desired. Since as a person he is absolute, he is not only the fruit of a common intention, but a testimony to the freedom of the gift, the guarantee of the solidity of the marriage vow, and the continuity of loving presence.

It is because he is the testimony of an unconditional gift that he cannot be the sole absolute and unique purpose of the home, the intended result of the bodily act. Only because the reciprocal gift of freedom is itself absolute and without conditions, the child can be respected as a subject.

But the risk of willing and desiring him is still a risk to the love of the two parents.

INTERACTION OF THE TWO ENDS OF MARRIAGE

The liberality of love conditions the liberality of love being objectified in the child. And the child does not completely develop as a subject, respected as such, unless he is accepted in the absolute unpredictability of what he will be as a subject—as a third. Even at worst, conjugal intimacy is often strengthened by the arrival of a mentally handicapped child. Intimacy and its unity, the child and his freedom as subject, are reciprocal conditions.

A similar largesse takes its place between the two ends of marriage. We have followed the genesis of human love and come to conjugal intimacy, beginning with the man-woman dialogue; along this path, we have concluded that the risk of the child, and the acceptance of his unpredictability as subject, a third person in the conjugal relationship, are the condition of the absolute largesse of love.[11]

We could have followed man's genesis in social life from the time of his appearance in a family. We would have found that the total genesis of a person requires knowing and being known, that one is never truly a person except within a personal relationship. And we could have arrived at the largesse of married love as the absolute condition for the true human genesis of the child. Man does not become really man except face to face with another, personal absolute where the fundamental relationship is revealed. Nothing can replace for the child the freely given love of his parents for each other, even if the cultural expression of that love leads to conflict, the Oedipus complex for example. There is no question of reducing oppositions—they will exist in proportion to the unity. Many people mistrust passion and its harshness; yet the worst danger is loving less in order to be undisturbed. It means at the same time to be less a man.

The two ends of marriage can be united: We should say it is the family, as a new reality, intersubjective and creative of intersubjectivity, that is the end of marriage. As a matter of fact, intimacy includes the two ends in germinal form, as the bodily expression of intersubjectivity and the actual point of its emergence.

[11] The unpublished lectures of Père Jacques Sommet have been particularly useful to me in analyzing this interaction of the two ends of marriage.

CHAPTER ELEVEN

The Frailty of Human Love

In setting our sights for the ideal, have we missed what is humbly and wonderfully possible? We have avoided all delusive rehearsals of the myth of Tristan; it is idle to make an absolute of the exceptional minutes in love or friendship when the curtain of solitude rises, and the world appears for a moment as it is, simply because we ourselves come close to what we are—one being for another. Those are the minutes that give life its essential zest. But while the humble and wonderful history of such a love achieved by two beings who live for one another is indeed the highest possible achievement, it is so rare that we must frankly examine failure, too, and study carefully the momentary or permanent weaknesses that make such failure possible.

Failure forever, or only for a day? Down the centuries, our songmakers have mingled and compared these two forms of happiness in all their certainty and frailty. The frailty of love is part of our own frailty, but the speed of social change has added the hazards of social, cultural, and institutional flux.

SOCIOLOGICAL CHANGES

Love has more freedom in an industrial society, but fewer walls to shelter its weakness. It is easier to commit one's life to the man or woman one loves when traditional images have become less imperious in imposing various functions on the couple which are beneficial to society but detrimental to their own role, intimacy.

The home itself has shrunk. It is normally reduced to the couple with its young children. The failure to integrate old people in modern society is, by the way, one of our most pressing social problems. The family includes only a few individuals of the same blood, and blood ties count for less and less. The patriarchal family grouped married sons and their wives and children under the authority of a single family head; the middle-class families of the early industrial age still exhibited a similar hierarchy. These families, guardians of culture, projected upon the whole people their own concepts of the couple, of "feminine" and "masculine." Our new independence of the land has freed the family of its roots in one locality. The family need no longer be large in order to insure its material well-being and the preservation of the family property. The stability of the "family home" has gradually lost importance.

For the family has become extremely mobile. Landed property is no longer a tie to the soil or to a fixed geographical location. It seems preferable to obtain it by one's own efforts. We love the parents' home no longer, we love the home we have established ourselves. Husbands or wives are chosen within constantly greater geographical and cultural areas. The ties of the family with other couples are based on friendship rather than kinship. Depending increasingly on its earnings and no longer on its patrimony, the family often still seeks to establish a center, a hearth, a bit of land, but the choice of location is no longer motivated by love of place itself.

The understanding of woman's role begins to broaden. Her actual situation is often ahead of the image that has lingered on. Woman tends more and more to take her place in society, according to personal functions and responsibilities that go far beyond her traditional role of housekeeper, teacher, and guardian of the hearth. There are fewer economic reasons for the father to wield authority over his wife and children.

All this brings with it greater instability. The traditional family was stable; its life centered on insuring the survival of the race and the family home. The children took their place in the succession. Today the family is far less organized. More centered on itself, the couple tries to space the birth of its children; it must do so, for its own sake as well as for them. In this concern, it can no longer turn to an ancestral home or to the clan. The marriage bond, then, seems more and more as a simple contract for life in common, which may be broken when circumstances change, subject only to normal contractual rules: it is valid only *sic rebus stantibus*, so long as circumstances remain the same.

The greater frangibility of this contract bears some relation to freedom in choosing a partner. The same social circumstances that favor a free choice without parental interference are also conducive to greater freedom in premarital relations, and contribute to the instability of marriage.

This development should not be downgraded; it creates its own new family ties. Sociologists describing the average levels of city industrial life speak of the "nuclear family." The evolution can broadly be described as a transition from "parental" to "conjugal"; that is, transition from a large group with close family relationships—which assure its survival by rigorous traditions even in the matter of transmitting life—to the married couple which joins two strangers in a history to be made by them alone. It involves also a transition from a reassuring tradition to risks assumed personally.

It is no accident that this development is accompanied in industrial society by the secularization of the world and marriage itself. A man who had his place in a large family group or in a tribe found himself more fully integrated in a world organized as a hierarchy, an orderly nature. For us the whole world now ceases to be a cosmos. The era of thundering theophanies is past; there are no sacred areas or places; everything is profane. At one time, the bonds that united man to the cosmos were reflected in the married couple; they were the foundation for the relations of man and woman; it then was easy, for example, to draw a parallel from the slow maturation of the unborn child to the pattern of woman's work and behavior. From microcosm to macrocosm, all symbols revealed the secrets of unity. The ties of the couple, physical and sensual or social and religious, were without break and without duality. Today, the couple tends to have only human ties; it no longer has a part in the sacred rites of cosmic cycles. With the ceremonies of agrarian civilization, man took his place in a universal order; he absorbed its meaning even as he accepted its traditions. No links to the past history of the race guide the couple any longer today as it faces life ahead. Its fate is wholly in its own hands, its future before it. The past no longer forms a reassuring continuum with the present. Of course, today man can go back thousands of years and retrace the early stages of his own biological evolution; but this scientific knowledge fails to adjust him to the world, nor does it place him in the world; he no longer knows his true place. He knows more about his own history, but it is no longer an orderly story. Being nowhere in the world, afloat, man places a higher value on the love he shares with one other; here a new dimension is most clearly revealed. The couple will create for itself a degree of private life that was unknown to the traditional group. In marriage the scale of values tips slowly from transmission of life for the benefit of the group to the discovery of true intimacy. Sensual values count for less than being-together, the compatibility of mind and spirit.[1] The transmission of life and the attitude toward children take on a new meaning because a greater responsibility for the children's education—more difficult and more freely assumed—rests more and more on the couple alone. Help in that education there may be, but it comes from a larger collectivity and directly from the state, not from the family. And self-discovery is hastened and is imperative in the proportion as man takes his place in a social fabric that is looser and less fixed.

But the transition from a family group strong in its own ties and rigid traditional organization, to a couple left to the tides of a larger history, calls for a multiplication of contacts, a wealth of human interdependence well beyond the limits of the family group. A slow universalization has been necessary, a concrete awareness of the humanity of all men, and the appearance of a language

---

[1] "The experience of what mind is . . . Ego that is 'we' . . . 'we' that is a single Ego." G. W. F. Hegel, *The Phenomenology of Mind*, J. B. Baillie, trans. (New York: Harper & Row, 1967), p. 227.

common to a greater number of men and of woman. Dialogues between them become possible, and sexuality itself may become its own means of communication.

The basic tie now is created by two strangers harmonizing their different vocabularies of childhood experiences that were their human genesis. At the same time society has established and prolonged an intermediate stage between childhood and adulthood—adolescence, the time of encounters and discoveries.[2]

In passing from tradition to voluntary risk—from the full presence lived by the group and perpetuated by it to the unknown future of a history yet to be created, from a fixed place in the social network to the shifting ground where incorporation in social life depends on energy and will power—the married man and woman in their intimacy are often more sensitized to the fragmentation of society than to the rising tide of more universal human relations.

It is within this new cultural framework that we must reinterpret the permanent weaknesses of human love.

PERMANENT THREATS

Certain ever-present dangers threaten love from within and cast a shadow over it. Others come from the child and can be a burden both on love and on the child.

Eroticism may be an expression of a love it does not originate, and its dynamism, beyond that of the species, reveals the force of a specifically human need, that of the "other as man," to use Karl Marx's term. More deeply still, Eros can become the language of intersubjectivity, showing in the bright light of love's bliss that man is truly spirit, that he is I-with-the-other, free of all dreams of interiority, illusions of an inner life, or the unhappy conscience of "beautiful souls." The lover has no refuge in himself; truly he is what he is before the other. Nevertheless the flaming letters in which human freedom can prompt Eros to write his own history compound the ambiguity of all language by compounding the

2 Cf. Peter Berger and Hansfried Kellner, "Le mariage ét la construction de la réalité," in *Diogenes*, No. 46 (April–June 1964), pp. 3–32.

symbolism. This performance, in effect, rises slowly from a distant realm outside of language; it already has its structure and in it we can read a design not of freedom but of the species. A design? Or a drift, a trend, a sort of statistical force which makes its way to a given point. Its sense may be lost even as we seem to have discerned its direction. The taste for pleasure remains—the male taste for the female, the female's powerful attraction to the male in all their veiled variations. But the call of the species can never be maintained except as filtered through childhood experience. It is precisely because the voice of the species is already transposed, socialized, historicized, that man is a man. But in becoming language, the charms and spells of these attractions, before marriage and in its early stages, conceal as much as they reveal the gift of self to the point of self-sacrifice. The gift is all too easy, and so is sincerity.

This passionate desire, this violent physical attraction is subject to the sudden breaks and slow regressions of eroticism. The sexual relation may become insipid, repetitive, even impossible. What then really remains of the one taste for the other as a human being? To condemn the couple to an intimacy that has become impossible makes marriage the instrument and cause of infidelity. Once beyond Eros' spell, all the demands for self-sacrifice come to light, but now it is too late. Nervous tension displaces intimacy, and separation is necessary. There are slower collapses, with ever rarer lucid moments of self-examination in which to realize the magnitude and progress of the rupture. Deprived of Eros' support, love wears out and founders in the labyrinth of life—in banality, indifference, and every degree of boredom, monotony, and dreary distaste.

In all this, the failure only ratifies an illusion. A man thought he was in love; he was merely caught in the snares of eroticism. He thought he loved as he made the same gestures as millions of others and because eroticism had become accepted as the language of love, at least when it prepares the way for marriage. And whether it is an extreme case, turning fascination into repulsion, or slow erosion and the staleness of habit—the interdependence of love and eroticism is evident. A mistake has been made in the erotic dialogue, just as it can be made in any other dialogue and mono-logue; he has been carried away by the symbols of Eros as others have been carried away by words.

But true love, those miraculous encounters in which lover and beloved are at last themselves, no longer alone, in the midst of the world of their love—cannot even such love be destroyed by violent and repeated assaults? Every morning the miracle begins anew, as fragile, as tormented by the world as ever, yet quiet and appeased. Then comes a day, though no jealousy or spite or bore-dom ever invaded the home, when the bond is loosened. Of course one still likes the other, but one no longer loves, or one loves someone else. While love is real, and expresses the human need of the other, while it is total and puts the lovers at each other's mercy, it still can wear away day after day in the slow round and sudden shocks of a history being made by two.

Those who have recovered from erotic illusions, or who have never known real love, have they not the right to ask: "If we were deceived by the language of Eros, or if the knot tied forever has slowly come apart, or if it has broken in spite of us, must we be forever bound by the promise of a day?"

The freedom of the individual may assert itself at any moment in unpredictable ways: I do not know and cannot know what I will want tomorrow. This is not in itself an insurmountable ob-stacle to definite commitments, but here my deepest subjectivity is involved and it is impossible for me to put the erotic impulse aside. How, then, can a man give himself entirely, every moment, without exposing himself and the other to the piercing doubt whether concrete fidelity can find its place, and gather strength, apart from the sexual relation?

Finally, the child, implicit in the mutual gift of the body, is himself a danger, especially in the sense that he can either threaten or strengthen the marriage bond. Parents joined in marriage and bound by this tie run the risk that the child may become the center of affection for one or the other. We shall not go into what con-flicts might arise from the "Oedipus" or "Electra" complexes, most pronounced when the family is most united.

We hear a great deal about the effects on the child of family disunity. Psychological difficulties and failures to integrate in society often arise here. But should we not give as much attention to the victims of a home kept stable only by a sense of duty? And how many are victims of the aimless promiscuity that takes the place of intimacy, or of the possessive love of a parent who has been deceived by his partner?

The marriage vow holds as many dangers for love as it holds promises. It does make bodily union the beginning and not the end; but it creates dangers which it does nothing to surmount; it gives ratification, but no help.

MUST DIVORCE BE ADMITTED?

If the marriage vow is equivocal, how can it be definitive? If it is not definitive, how can it guarantee that, at the very moment when the lovers give themselves to each other, their love is such that each is really willing to accept self-sacrifice in the realization of his or her fundamental relation to the other?

How to escape from this vicious circle? The vow makes love a free act, but that act itself is based more or less consciously on sexual attraction, and this attraction can prompt a man to promise more than a man's will can carry out. Love can be an illusion. Under its spell, how can a vow limit one's freedom, even if the true gift of love is willing to accept the sacrifice of self? And how can it be love unless there is willingness to make this gift total and irrevocable? The vow intended to be final increases the difficulties, but it does not increase the chances of success.

Free love is no solution, because here Eros is at the service of the other. From the heights of love one falls back into erotic play and mythical dreams, or simply into the prison of selfishness. The lovers may of course find their own road amid the determinisms and snares of the history in which they have already become engaged—we get out of an impasse as best we can. But the difficulty here comes from a factor external to nascent love, and the exceptions cannot be considered rules.

We must consider the development of love itself to decide whether the vow should be interpreted in a more flexible way. The vow is necessary; the love of the couple is handed over to society because they wish to create a history. Lovers rarely brief themselves by consulting the divorce laws in case of unexpected failure. Their hope of daily progress in the history of their love is a near certainty, and any new assurance, any promise seems eminently desirable. But once failure has come and is obvious to all, must a man drag along in chains, to protect institutions which often serve to screen interests that cannot always be admitted—institutions which compel the sacrifice of self and of the other? We were in love, but the other has left, and life goes on one gray day after another. After the first despair, interest in life and in the world slowly returns. Should we not triumph over the past and cease to live on memories?

If the couple may not go back on their original choice without lapsing into the ambiguities of free love and so denying their deep need of wholeness, there remains recourse to that society to which they had entrusted their love to make it an institution. Society, the witness of their love, will be the judge of its failure. This is not a return to individualism. Marriage would remain an institution, the vow final for husband and wife. They would not be their own judges. The society to which they have delivered their love would be the judge of its defeat, and could in certain cases grant divorce.[3]

[3] Not that divorce seems desirable; on the contrary, it is most often a tribute to monogamy, or, more precisely, to the perfection expected of marriage. In most divorces the couple has judged, not that marriage is unimportant, but that it has failed to reach the desired perfection and that this perfection is unattainable in future with the same partner. An effort is then made to create a new union in which intimacy comes closer to the ideal. If the requirements of intimacy are clear, divorce can appear only as the lesser of two evils. And it is only as a lesser evil that it will be tolerated by a society, which is aware that conjugal intimacy with all its demands remains the source and initiator of all social life. Here again we must emphasize that our analysis is limited and does not include the other sources, and social foundations of the institution of marriage—we have kept to the point of view of intimacy. Finally, the Church, in making marriage a sacrament, a matter we shall discuss in the following pages, has given particular attention to the coordination of sacramental reality with the requirements of intimacy and the standards of society.

MARRIAGE AS A SACRAMENT

The institution of marriage as a sacrament provides support to human love in such a way that it derives its strength from within. The vow that makes the choice irrevocable, and love of the other even when this means sacrifice of self, rest on the very model of this love: the love of Christ for his Church.

We do not claim transcendence; there is no question of calling God as a third party to aid the lovers. My partner who constitutes my humanity is not a simple reflection of a fantastic demiurge, and my happiness is not in the beyond. The only point of reference is the other, the loved one who is close by, and Christ has no other face; he reveals himself only in the ties of intersubjectivity, in ways that are forever unexpected. The reference to Christ universalizes love, yet leaves it completely concrete and individual, and incorporates it into the Mystical Body. The foundation of love becomes Charity, just as the Mystical Body becomes the inner foundation of intersubjectivity. Charity begins with the one who is closest, and includes kissing the leper no less than embracing my marriage partner—on condition that in each case the kiss is inspired by love and not given out of a sense of duty. Again the choice is for what is most human;—joy and the willingness to overcome all difficulties. There is no room here for masochistic fantasies in which some tyrannical God asserts his power by degrading us, or a transcendent Being who manifests himself in its unique substance within our knowledge of nothingness. We are speaking of a God truly become man, a God who universalized his presence by his own death and resurrection. Human love is rooted in Christ, who can never be apprehended except in the other, and who makes of intimacy itself a new language, the sign of his authentic presence, his reality.

Sexual desire becomes an secondary expression of the supernatural. We have seen human love press eroticism into its service and transform it into an expression of intersubjectivity; just so, on the supernatural level, charity turns human love into the expression of a higher interdependence, a more universal and authentic relationship, a single body that is necessary so that each may become truly himself, a member of the Body of Christ.

We may retrace the path of love in reverse and consider the experience of St. John of the Cross as merely a form of eroticism, because the language he used is that of lovers; or, we can orient the entire area of eroticism in the direction of its own transcendence, if we believe with Teilhard de Chardin that everything is supported from above.

A sexuality cut off from all of human existence fails to reach the other who is involved; it fails to reach him whom it pursues. But through sexuality, human love is at times able to accomplish, on its own level, what had been planned along different lines. A loftier love can triumph over the shortcomings of human love and fulfill its promises. The correspondence between charity and sexuality reveals its full meaning, beyond its own contradictions. The truth of sexuality lies in going beyond it, not in trying to avoid it. Sexuality reveals to man his fundamental dimension. He is for the other or he does not exist. Human love reveals to man that he is nothing apart of intersubjectivity. Marriage as a sacrament can also reveal to him a meaning of this "nothing" and of being "for the other" that is transcendent, concrete, and universal, provided he truly counts himself as nothing in loving the one who is closest to him as Christ loved his Church—unto death.

For failure in marriage is like dying to oneself and not like a new start. It is the very radicalism of love that makes it Christian. In accepting marriage as a sacrament, the Christian certainly does not want unhappiness in love—quite the contrary—but he prefers to lose and die of his loss rather than accept failure or seek solutions other than pursuit of the same love. Not to admit that love has met with defeat simply because it continues only on one side can be more terrible than death. What is at stake for him is loving to the point of preferring to die rather than give up loving, of forcing his love on the other if he should try to escape, of delivering over to the other the very life he threatens to take away—a life that the other would perhaps much prefer to see directed, modified, and resumed in less passionate areas.

Intimacy can reveal fundamental intersubjectivity to those who love. Intersubjectivity experienced in the sacrament of marriage can be a concrete revelation of Christ living in the Mystical Body. Or, to employ a better, more traditional phrase, intimacy in turn can reveal "the truth of the Body of Christ," and cast light upon the basic essential of progress toward the goal where eroticism speaks of love, and love of charity.

BIBLIOGRAPHY

Bailey, D. S. *The Man-Woman Relation in Christian Thought.* London: Longmans Green, 1959.
————. *The Mystery of Love and Marriage.* New York: Harper & Brothers, 1952.
Beauvoir, Simone de. *The Second Sex.* New York: Alfred A. Knopf, 1953; Bantam Books, 1961.
Brown, Norman O. *Life Against Death: The Psychoanalytic Meaning of History.* Middletown, Conn.: Wesleyan University Press, 1959.
————. *Love's Body.* New York: The Macmillan Co., 1966.
Fairbairn, W. R. D. *Psychoanalytic Studies of the Personality.* London: Tavistock, 1962. 2d ed.
Fiedler, Leslie. *Love and Death in the American Novel.* New York: Meridian, 1962.
Ford, C. S., and Beach, F. A. *Patterns in Sexual Behavior.* New York: Harper & Brothers, 1951.
Friedan, Betty. *The Feminine Mystique.* New York: W. W. Norton, 1963.
Guntrip, Harry. *Personality Structure and Human Interaction.* London, Hogarth Press, 1961.
Hampson, J. L. and Hampson, Joan. "The Ontogenesis of Sexual Behavior in Man," in W. C. Young, ed., *Sex and Internal Secretions.* 3d ed.; Baltimore: Williams & Wilkins, 1961, Vol. 2, pp. 1401–1432.
Horney, Karen. *New Ways in Psychoanalysis.* New York: W. W. Norton, 1939. Chapter on "Feminine Psychology."
Johann, R. *The Meaning of Love.* Westminster, Md.: Newman Press, 1959.
Laing, R. D. *The Divided Self.* London, Tavistock, 1960.
————. *The Self and Others.* London, Tavistock, 1962.
Macmurray, John. *Reason and Emotion.* London, Faber, 1961. 2d ed.
————. *Persons in Relation.* New York: Harper & Brothers, 1961.
Marcuse, Herbert. *Eros and Civilization.* London: Routledge & Kegan Paul, 1956.
Marx, Engels, Lenin, and Stalin. *The Woman Question.* New York: International Publishers, 1951.

Maslow, A. H. "Dominance, Personality, and Social Behavior in Women." *J. Soc. Psych.*, Vol. 10 (1939), pp. 3-39.

————. "Self-esteem (dominance-feeling) and Sexuality in Women." *J. Soc. Psych.*, Vol. 16 (1942), pp. 259-94.

Mead, Margaret. *Sex and Temperament in Three Primitive Societies.* New York: Apollo, 1935.

————. *From the South Seas.* New York. Morrow, 1939.

Merleau-Ponty, M. *Phenomenology of Perception.* London: Routledge & Kegan Paul, 1962. Particularly chapter 5, "The Body in Its Sexual Being."

Noonan, John T., Jr. *Contraception.* Cambridge, Mass.: Harvard University Press, 1965.

Ramsay, Paul. "Sartre: Sex in Being," in *Nine Modern Moralists.* Englewood Cliffs, N. J.: Prentice-Hall, 1962.

Rieff, Phillip. *Freud, The Mind of the Moralist.* London: Gollanz, 1959.

Sullivan, Dan. "Sex and the Person," in *Commonweal,* July 22 (1966), pp. 460-64.

Women in the New Asia. Barbara Ward, ed. Paris: UNESCO, 1964.

Watts, Alan. *Nature, Man, and Woman.* London, Thames & Hudson, 1958.

Format by Katharine Sitterly
Set in Linotype Electra
Composed, printed and bound by The Haddon Craftsmen, Inc.
HARPER, & ROW, PUBLISHERS, INCORPORATED